The Traveler's Guide to Native America

The Great Lakes Region

By Hayward Allen

Foreword by Pemina Yellow Bird

NORTHWORD
PRESS, INC
P.O. Box 1360, Minocqua, WI 54548

Library of Congress Cataloging-in-Publication Data

Allen, Hayward.
    The traveler's guide to Native America : the Great Lakes region /
by Hayward Allen and Pemina Yellow Bird.
        p.   cm.
    Includes index.
    ISBN 1-55971-139-6
    1. Indians of North America–Great Lakes Region–Antiquities-
-Guidebooks. 2. Historic sites–Great Lakes Region–Guidebooks.
3. Great Lakes Region–Antiquities–Guidebooks. 4. Great Lakes
Region–Description and travel–Guidebooks.   I. Yellow Bird,
Pemina.   II. Title.
E78.G7A45 1992
917.704'33–dc20   92-9426
                                                                          CIP

CREDITS

Front cover photograph: Peggy Morsch

Inside photographs
Barb Schoenherr Photography, pp. 4, 8, 12, 16, 18, 21, 27, 34, 36, 38, 47, 48, 52, 57, 58, 59, 64, 66, 67, 74, 78, 80, 81, 88, 90, 94, 98, 101, 102, 106, 110, 113, 114, 117, 118, 121, 122, 125, 126, 130, 133, 134, 137, 139, 141, 142, 143, 144, 145, 147, 148, 150, 151, 153, 154, 155, 159, 178, 179, 180, 181, 182, 184, 188, 191; National Park Service/Effigy Mounds National Monument/Allan Zarling, pp. 15, 22; Jack Blosser/Ohio Historical Society, p. 24; The Scioto Society, Inc./*Tecumseh!*, pp. 28, 51; First Frontier Inc./*Blue Jacket*/Pamela Hershey, p. 30; SunWatch Archaeological Park, p. 31; *Trumpet in the Land*, p. 32; William Hammond Mathers Museum/Indiana University, p. 42; Angel Mounds State Historic Site/Indiana Department of Natural Resources, pp. 45, 46; Mounds State Park/Indiana Department of Natural Resources, p. 54; Eiteljorg Museum of American Indian and Western Art, pp. 55, 56; Cahokia Mounds State Historic Site, p. 62; Starved Rock State Park/Illinois Department of Conservation, p. 68; Illinois Department of Commerce and Community Affairs, p. 73; Marquette Mission Park and Museum of Ojibwa Culture, pp. 84, 95, 97; Teysen's Historical Museum, pp. 86, 87; State Archives of Michigan, p. 92; Richard Sparks/National Park Service, pp. 162, 175; Great Lakes Indian Fish and Wildlife Commission, pp. 164, 165; Robert W. Baldwin, p. 167; St. Louis County Historical Society, Duluth, MN, pp. 169, 170, 173; M. Budak/Minnesota Historical Society, p. 176

Maps
Mary Shafer, pp. 41, 61, 87, 108-109, 161, 187

© 1992 Hayward Allen. All rights reserved.
Published by NorthWord Press, Inc.
Box 1360, Minocqua, WI 54548

Edited by Greg Linder
Consulting Editor: Pemina Yellow Bird
Designed by Russell S. Kuepper
Primary Photographer: Barb Schoenherr

For a free catalog describing NorthWord's
line of nature books and gifts, call 1-800-336-5666

ISBN 1-55971-139-6

Table of Contents

Foreword

I was born and, for part of my life, raised on the Fort Berthold Indian Reservation. I am an enrolled member of the Three Affiliated Tribes: the Mandan, Hidatsa, and Arikara Nations. We once lived along the banks of the upper Missouri River in large earthlodge villages, where we grew corn, beans, squash, and tobacco, and hunted the buffalo and other game. We lived within a highly complex society that was guided by our living religion.

With the onset of the white man and his diseases, there began a holocaust among our people that decimated our tribes and left us with a national sorrow that time has not healed. Next came his laws. We were forced to move onto allotted lands and out of our close, communal society. Then, with the construction of the Garrison Dam upon our grandfather, the Missouri River, our beautiful homelands were flooded to make electricity for the white man. These changes, along with many others not of our choosing, proved catastrophic and destructive to the fabric of our rich culture and society.

Sadly, this situation is not unique to the Three Affiliated Tribes. There is not a single indigenous nation that has remained unscarred since the coming of the white man to our country. These are the things I want you to know before you come to our homes. These are the things we have had to endure so that you could have a home.

* * * * *

With that rather sober beginning, then, I will say that I am grateful to Hayward Allen for giving me the opportunity to write the preface to his book. You have this book in your hands because you are considering a journey into Native lands; I feel fortunate to have your attention before that journey begins, because I have been given a chance to share with you some viewpoints you won't get anywhere else but from an indigenous person. Please keep in mind that you are reading my viewpoint and opinions; I do not pretend to speak for every person in my tribe, let alone other tribes and their members. These comments are offered in the spirit of sharing with you my perceptions of our history, a vantage point that non-Indians seldom get. It is my hope that you will receive the comments in the same spirit.

As these chapters were being written, Hayward very bravely brought them to my house, where epic battles ensued over the archaelogical information included about each tribe. A compromise was struck: The information stayed in the book, and I got to write the preface! In some cases, such as the sections on the moundbuilders of Ohio and Illinois, the archaelogical information is the

A statue of the Winnebago warrior, Red Bird, stands beneath dramatic skies near the shore of Lake Winnebago.

only information given, because there are no longer tribes that live in these states, much less tribes that build mounds in that way.

Archaeologists would have us believe that these tribes are now extinct. It's my belief, however, that descendants of these mound builders survive today among many indigenous nations. And therein lies the rub: Scientists, through their own paradigms and value systems–i.e., scientific study–have drawn many conclusions and made many guesses that are erroneously taken as fact by many American citizens. Further, it is my opinion that the image many American citizens have of indigenous peoples is one that was created by archaeologists, anthropologists, historians, and museum professionals, and the image is thus necessarily distorted and incorrect. History is written by the conquerors of this world, and American history is no exception.

Some indigenous people, including myself, go so far as to say that these disciplines are, by their very nature, ethnocentric and institutionally racist. To say that you are going to study a group of people with their full consent and detailed knowledge and understanding of your operations and intent is one thing. To arbitrarily enter their domain without their permission or consent or full knowledge of your intentions, and to record your observations with an eye biased by your very upbringing and personal value system is quite another thing indeed. To put it bluntly, indigenous people are tired of the dominant culture telling them who they are and what they are all about. Moreover, we are tired of seeing the dominant culture being taken more seriously when it speaks about us than *we* are when we speak about us. Indigenous peoples, more than any other group, are eminently qualified to teach others about their history, their homelands, their opinions, and their issues. If you give us half a chance, you will see that we are able to do just that. What we have to say may make some feel uncomfortable, but it will be an accurate portrayal of Indian country, past and present.

Do not be alarmed if you encounter some passionate native people who may tell you some of these same things as you travel through Indian country. Do not take offense; they have suffered more than you can know. If I could give you any advice as you undertake your journey, it would be to keep an open mind and heart; abandon what you have heard and been taught about native people; make up your own mind. Try not to make value judgments as you look at humble houses with junk cars in the yards. Try to remember that these are people who were forced to live in a value system that is both foreign and hateful to them, people who fight to hang onto their own. Under the best of circumstances, trust must be established before true communication begins; I believe you can understand why some indigenous people find it hard to trust.

A little respect goes a long way, and in Indian country it's no different. Ladies, if you are at a powwow and you don't see any of the local women wearing a bikini top and short shorts, it would be a good idea to leave yours at the hotel. Little things like that are important. Try to look around you. Get a feel for how others are behaving, and act accordingly. Then you'll do just fine.

One final topic: Many areas in Indian country are considered holy and sacred. In fact, it is said that all lands are holy and sacred, since they sustain life. Our relatives, the rocks, the green rooted things, the four-leggeds, the winged ones, the water beings, those that crawl upon the Earth, and us, the two-leggeds, are all alive today because of our Mother the Earth.

For our purposes, however, my remarks are aimed at those areas that have been used in a sacred way and are in all likelihood still being used that way today. I am also speaking of those areas of our Mother the Earth that cradle the bodies of our ancestors.

As you would accord respect to the Vietnam War's Wall of Names; as you would be moved to silence and respect as you watch John F. Kennedy's eternal flame; so, too, must you behave at public sites that speak of our ancestors or contain their final resting places.

Don't walk on top of burial mounds or pick up those things you may find there: Those things belong to the spirits. You may encounter public parks that have the bodies and personal burial belongings of Indian people on display. These things hurt us to our core, and I ask you to turn away from these places. When you get home, please write to your Congressmen and women, asking them to close sites like these and return our ancestors to their rest. If you know that you are in a sacred place–for instance, Bear Butte in South Dakota–have respect for the indigenous people who come there to pray for their people.

Take a moment to pray yourself–for your family, for your country, for the Earth–for you are in the presence of power.

I wish for you a safe journey, the opportunity to grow and learn as you travel in Indian country, and many smiling faces and much good news to greet you upon your return home.

–Pemina Yellow Bird

Introduction

Whiteness came back to the paths after each
footstep and the travelers
never met in the single files
who deepened the same shadows.
  – W.S. Merwin, "The Prints"

More than three centuries before the poet Merwin, Francis Bacon wrote: "Travel in the younger sort is a part of education; in the elder, a part of experience. He that traveleth into a country before he hath some entrance into the language goeth to school, and not to travel."

The world's greatest writers have praised the virtues of traveling to new places, seeing new sights, meeting different people, sampling the cultures of other nations and other times. Anyone who has traveled beyond the place where he or she was born knows the thrill and the fear of going someplace new, as well as the wonder and glory of discovering a place for oneself.

The "Origins" series has been designed with the education of the traveler in mind. We hope to introduce to each reader dimensions of our continental history that are different from those presented in other travel guides.

Because this is the first volume of "Origins," it has been a special experience for the author. I must confess to a fundamental ignorance of the heritage that surrounds us in the Midwest. In school, the history books told us bits and pieces about the role that American Indian nations have played in shaping the destiny of this continent, but even these pieces were mostly negative and demeaning.

Because this book focuses on discovery, education, experience, and enhanced understanding, my eyes have been opened to a different vista, thanks to my Native American friends–especially Pemina Yellow Bird and Michael Yellow Bird–and to the myriad sources of information leading beyond personal contact and experience. Through the hindsight that history affords, for example, I learned about different and conflicting perceptions of geography, religion, human relations, and the pressure that time places upon people to take from others what is not theirs.

It would be innacurate to say that only the European nations were cruel in their acts of territorial expansion for, long before the 16th century, smaller and weaker Native American nations were being pushed away from their homelands by stronger, larger ones. Here, one sees dramatic parallels with the cultures of Europe, which were warring with one another at basically the same time.

To say that the coming of Columbus to this hemisphere dramatically

Spearpoints from the prehistoric Wisconsin site known as Aztalan.

9

changed the inter-national wars here is certainly an understatement. New technologies, new political and religious dictates, new concepts of wealth, new diseases, new perceptions of time and space, and a seemingly endless chain of people crossed the Atlantic in the brief span of three centuries. The collision of cultures was both horrific and magnificent.

As Pemina writes, "There is not a single indigenous nation that has remained unscarred since the coming of the white man to our country." *The Traveler's Guide* does not avoid this confrontation. However, the primary intention of our series is not only to acknowledge this reality, but also to suggest ways that all travelers on this planet can learn from one another.

How to Use This Guide

The first chapter lays down a foundation, discussing the earlier inhabitants of the Great Lakes area–the "Ancient Ones." The information is important because it will be reflected in later sections on Ohio, Indiana, and Illinois. In these three states, what one can see today tells only of the past, so some understanding of that past is essential. Information about the Paleo-Indian, the Archaic Indian, and the Adena-Hopewell-Temple Mound Builder cultures is important in understanding the sites that are available for visitation.

When the traveler is in certain areas of Michigan, Wisconsin, or Minnesota, this knowledge is also important. Similarly, it's critical to realize that, while archaeologists and anthropologists have a sense of time, place, cultures, and peoples, the descendants of the Ancient Ones also have a living, preserved perspective about the Great Lakes region. The two visions may at times seem incompatible, but it's possible to learn from both.

Each of the sites and special attractions mentioned in the guide are, in one way or another, Native American in intent. Whenever it's possible or relevant, chapters are constructed along a historical timeline. Thus the traveler is led through a state's development, and places or people are pointed out along the way if they are important to what can be seen today.

In these pages, the traveler might read about a mound site, a dramatic performance, or a collection of artifacts in a local historical society. The traveler is also introduced to colleges where courses are offered in Native American studies, and to specific events honoring the role that Indians played in the history of a county or a town.

If I were to recommend a step-by-step plan for experiencing "origins," it might go something like this:

1) Read about the area you're visiting, even if what you're reading is a public document, a private promotional piece, or a government publication. Pinpoint sites and events that have a Native American focus.

2) If you have time, read one or two histories of the area, and talk with an American Indian about your trip. Ask questions, listen, respond, and respect this person's point of view.

3) Go on your trip. Absorb what you see. Take notes, if you have the time and the inclination. Look at things beyond the sign that summarizes the display. In most cases, such signs are written by people who have a traditional, scientific, and/or Western point of view, so they may not reflect the reality of the display–especially if there is a spiritual meaning involved. If there is a published guide about the site, read the guide. Look long, and then think about your own life, your daily work, your religion and education. It's surprising how many connections can be made between our own lives and the lives of people who lived centuries and generations ago.

4) When you return home, seek out answers to the questions that have arisen during your trip.

5) Finally, know that when you read an article, watch a television program or a movie, take part in a conversation, or make a decision, your travel experiences will have some relevance. From time to time, they may even influence you profoundly. On these occasions, you have indeed discovered the primary reason for examining "origins."

This volume is simply a first step on a journey that you will undertake for yourself. We hope the guide will help you arrive at a better understanding of our continent's Native American heritage, and an appreciation of the necessity for supporting its preservation.

Additional Sources of Information

As you travel, public libraries can serve as a primary source of information about places to visit. State governments also provide extensive travel information, generally through an agency called the "Division of Tourism" or something similar. These agencies generally maintain toll-free numbers and information centers at major state and site entrances. If you're already at a site and you want to know more about it, try the local library, county historical society, or chamber of commerce. These institutions are generally eager to share information about their locale.

1
Times of the Ancient Ones

The area of the United States now confined within the borders of the Great Lakes states of Ohio, Indiana, Illinois, Michigan, Wisconsin, and Minnesota is in reality a geologic and glacial phenomenon that has been conducive to human habitation since the Wisconsin Glacier began its retreat some 10,000 years ago. At about the same time, aboriginal immigrants began to enter the territory being "evacuated" by the mile-thick ice-pack.

One might envision the exciting environment the immigrants encountered. Instead of an invisible state line marked only by welcoming signs, the border between what we know as Wisconsin and Illinois may have been a wall of ice more than a mile high. During the great glacial period between 80,000 B.C. and 8,000 B.C., this would have been a southern edge of the continent-wide Wisconsin Glacier. The ensuing tidal epoch began as the ice melted.

Thousands of years elapsed before the literal flood of water settled into what are now lakes and rivers, and thousands more passed before what was marshland became dry, rolling plains, valleys, and sloughs. Illinois was at the center of the flowage process, and this perhaps explains why there is little evidence of the Paleo-Indians of 12,000 years ago within what is now the "Prairie State."

As the ice retreated, generations passed. Cascading waterfalls built great rivers, and thousands of sculpted lakebeds were occupied by wildlife eager to recapture migratory feeding grounds. In its wake, the glacier deposited a half-dozen different kinds of churned soil, so trees and grasses of all kinds found fertile ground. Without question, the lower shores of the Great Lakes were ideal for the people who came to settle there and search for food and resources.

As early as 10,000 B.C., hunters had roamed the Upper Great Lakes region. At least 15,000 habitation sites have been located, including some yielding chipped-stone spear points similar to those found as far west as what is now New Mexico. Scholars call these first residents "Paleo-Indians," and it appears that their lives were centered around the quest for the great beasts–mastodons and mammoths–that lived along the edge of the Wisconsin Glacier.

With the demise of the dominant ice environment–lasting about 3000 years–there evolved a more permanent community, subsequently called the "Aqua-Plano" people. What distinguishes them from the Paleo-Indians is the evidence that they were more residential, using tools to hunt and fish as the seasons dictated. Their era was almost as extensive as that of their predecessors.

From about 5000 B.C. until 500 B.C., the western Great Lakes were enjoyed by two very specific cultures, the "Boreal Archaic" and the "Old

The recreated stockade at the Aztalan site resembles a frontier fort.

Copper." Both were interested in wood and stone fabrication. The Copper cultural faction emigrated north into what is now Canada, but the Boreal group, as the name implies, was woodland-dependent. The descendants of these people would become the Woodland Indians and would inhabit the expanse of the Great Lakes region.

There are many parallels between the Old Copper culture and the people who were living at the time in what is now Mexico. Both practiced farming, even to the point of growing flint corn, and both adopted similar practices in toolmaking, construction, and creating pottery. What is most significant, however, is the essential permanence of their settlements, as revealed by the tradition of mound building. The people moved from place to place seasonally, probably in accordance with the food resources available at different times of the year. Campsites have been located, but there is sufficient evidence to indicate that semi-permanent communities were also established. Tools and weapons were fashioned from flint, but tools made from granite have also been found. It's thought that the Archaic cultures began to develop trade routes in their regions, and there are indications that their spiritual lives included elements present in the later cultures of the Woodland peoples.

Apparently this spiritual connection was preserved through the centuries in the same way that the religions of other cultures have been transferred from generation to generation. Generally, the traveler becomes aware of this continuum only by studying collections held by museums or historical societies, these designed for non-Indian viewers and students. There are other narrations, however, provided by Native American histories. Native American visitors to historic places will find a heritage confirmed by tribal elders. Other perceptive travelers may find themselves following something akin to railroad tracks headed toward antique times but made of two different metals. One track is European, and the other consists of the native recollection of origination.

When the so-called Archaic cultures began to generate processed pottery and to grow seasonal crops, there was greater motivation to create permanent settlements. The ability to control resources enhances the desire to establish residence. However, it's also true that the natural world has a way of burying the past, much as the sands of time covered the magnificent bodies of the dinosaurs. The early Woodland Indian cultures are better known to us today than the Archaic cultures, because the evidence indicating their presence has not yet been totally consumed.

There were three groups whose fundamental recognition is based upon earthen mounds that remain today: the Adena, the Hopewell, and the Mississippian-Temple Mound Builders.

Some of these earthworks were built for defense, others for symbology, and others for the sacred burial of the dead. In fact, archaeologically speaking, the people of the "final" prehistoric period have been designated the Effigy Mound People.

Bird effigy mounds like these were built as a tribute to the birds of the area.

Adena Culture

The traveler will have to look beyond a name in order to locate the historic settlements and sites of the Adena culture. There is a small town in Ohio called Adena. It may have been named after the historic culture, but there is no other apparent, explicit connection. The early Native American culture itself was actually named after a mansion! Ohio's first gubernatorial residence, located near present-day Chillicothe, was called Adena, again related by name only to the region's earliest residents, though there were a number of mounds on the estate when the house was built, and many still survive.

Quite honestly, we have no way of knowing what the mound builders called themselves. It's possible, though, that they followed the culture-centric pattern of saying that they were "The First People," or simply "The People."

The Adena were hunter-gatherers who built circular houses with mud wattle walls and thatched roofs. Their mounds were conical or dome-shaped and were apparently made larger and larger as the years passed, or perhaps as the population grew. Initially, the mounds were burial mounds, log-lined tombs that were layered over the years. "Sacred Circles" of smaller, protective mounds were often erected around the tomb sites. The Adena people also constructed effigy mounds, shaped to represent totemic beings or images, such as serpents, bears, birds, and other animals. The artifacts within such mounds commonly include what is considered body armor made of stone or copper; jewelry made of pearl beads or mica; stone pipes; masks; and tools made of wood, bone, stone, and copper. Adena pottery is decorated with a series of cuts or with stamped images of natural objects. The cloth that has survived is made of vegetable fibers.

In the early days of archaeology, as scientists sought to understand the meaning of the mounds that were being "discovered" across the American midwest, no thought was given to the possibility that the mounds were sacred, holy sites that should not be disturbed. For many Native Americans, the exhuming of graves and burial sites provokes considerable agitation or remorse. While non-Indians might relate to the affront of digging up remains from Christian cemeteries, to Native Americans such actions can imply more than disrespect for the dead. Burials were a spiritual reunification with

An example of early Native American pottery.

essential elements of life, both the good and the bad, and the entering or disturbing of a grave can release spirits that were not meant to be released, according to many Native Americans. The Old Ones who have been disturbed on Earth are also disturbed in the spirit world, and must wander between the two worlds, pitifully lost.

In America, as in Europe, Egypt, and places where the Greek and Roman cultures thrived, archaeologists have pillaged and looted indiscriminately, drawing in their inquiry no distinction between the sacred and the profane, between what was of great spiritual significance and what was merely a community dumping ground for discarded pots, battered utensils, or the refuse of a nation defeated in war.

As a result, what we know about the Adena Culture is discerned from the collections and theories of 19th- and 20th-century archaeologists and anthropologists. Today, the collections are scattered about the country in private and public exhibits. Some lie dormant in boxes and crates within storage areas. The vast wealth and complexity of a culture that existed for so many centuries have gone the way of other ancient civilizations. Time and the elements have taken their toll, as have succeeding peoples who inhabited the Adena homelands and destroyed what cultural vestiges remained. Now the mounds are the primary monuments of the civilization that built them.

Hopewell Culture

The Hopewell cultural grouping was named after a farmer who owned land near Chillicothe, Ohio, where a massive cluster of mounds was located. However, the sphere of Hopewell influence extends from the Great Plains to the Mississippi Delta, north beyond the Great Lakes, and east to the Atlantic as well. The Hopewell ranged so widely that some anthropologists think the "culture" too expansive to be considered a single group. We can surmise, at least, that smaller sub-cultures would have formed as groups became acclimated to living in specific regions.

For a period of about five centuries, the Adena and Hopewell peoples coexisted in the same areas of the Ohio Valley and south of lakes Erie and Ontario. As mound building peoples, the two cultures overlap. The Hopewell people built larger mounds and, in some cases, erected their earthworks on top of Adena mounds. This practice may have occurred as a result of a merging with the Adena culture around 200 A.D., or perhaps it was due to emigration of the Adena to other parts of the continent. Mounds built on top of other burial sites are called "rider burials." Later tribes would build temples on many of the Hopewell mounds.

The Adena lived in relatively small communities, whereas the Hopewell were known to live in quite large groups. For example, one Hopewell site in

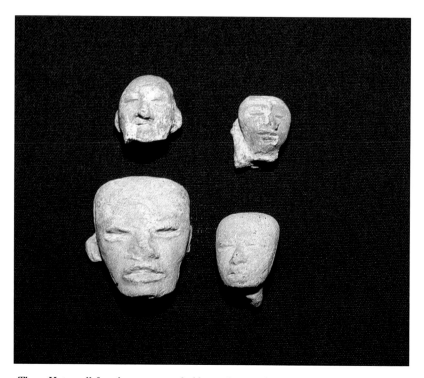

These Hopewell figurines were probably used as trade items between 200 B.C. and 500 A.D.

Ohio covers four square miles, and is literally filled with several layers of earthworks. In southern Illinois, there is a gigantic pyramid surrounded by earthworks that is thought to have been the site of a community containing many thousands of people.

The Hopewell culture was diverse, encompassing several complex levels of arts and crafts as well as spiritual and social developments. Artisans worked in different styles, ranging from abstract to concrete to realistic images. They created elaborate headdresses, cups made from conch shells, weapons fabricated of obsidian. Jewelry makers used pearls and gold, and made mirrors of mica. Potters made many kinds of objects and containers with clay. From the materials used—which came from as far away as the Rocky Mountains and the Caribbean Sea—it's obvious that an elaborate trade circuit was part of Hopewell life.

There is the question of natural resources available to those who lived in the Ohio Valley. As the population increased, so did the need for space and resources. One of the chief characteristics of the Woodland Indians is the cyclical or seasonal movement that allows them to take advantage of natural harvests. They then emigrate to an entirely different area and begin the circular movement again.

No one knows why the Hopewell culture came to an end, if indeed it did. There is a period of "empty" archaeological time, however, during which these early Woodland Indians presumably advanced to the tribal groupings later distinguished in the pre-Columbian era. There are many theories to explain the culture's "disappearance"–wars within the groups, diseases or epidemics, and even the theory that cultures and civilizations, like animal and plant species, have a lifetime and then naturally become extinct.

The Mississippian or Temple Mound Builders

The Temple Mound Builders (700 A.D. until about 1200) are considered the descendants of the Hopewell in the Ohio Valley. Their practices and social structure evidence many similarities to those of the Adena and Hopewell, including the construction of mounds. The Temple or Upper Mississippian Mound Builders had a lasting and critical cultural impact on the Great Lakes area.

If one is searching for mounds and earthworks, it is important to recognize that the establishment of that long-ago civilization was a slow process of emigration northward from the delta of the Mississippi. It was an up-river haul, and it took centuries to buck the mighty currents of the Mississippi and its tributaries. There are mounds to be found, mostly in the Minneapolis-St. Paul area and along the riverbanks that separate Minnesota from Wisconsin. These are not so far removed from their southern antecedents, however, that they have lost touch with the source of the Temple Mound Builder's way of life, which appears to have begun in what is now Central America.

The mounds reveal much about cultural evolution and migration, particularly as they address the end of earthly life. The templar design, similar to the step pyramids of Mexico and Guatemala, is joined by ceremonial pottery and masks that have been excavated, complete with inscriptions of skulls, bones, and weeping eyes. There are indications that the sacrifice of lives might have been another connection to the continuation of southern religious practices.

What appears to distinguish the Temple Mound Builders from the Adena and Hopewell peoples is an increased concern about death and afterlife. However, one must be cautious in interpreting evidence and must avoid assuming that their predecessors did not have a similarly profound regard for the afterlife. If one examines contemporary Native American spirituality, it's possible to find significant links with early ancestral beliefs and practices. While earthen temples may no longer be the means of expression, the interpretations of post-earthly existence retain a certain constancy.

The most dramatic demonstration of the extent of the Temple Mound

Builders' culture is the community of Cahokia, which is located near St. Louis and which was established more than 1,000 years ago. It was named for Cahokia Creek, which establishes a boundary for the community. The place is so remarkable that it's on UNESCO's "World Heritage List," a singular distinction. *National Geographic* has called this site "the crown jewel of Mississippian culture."

The 1990 U.S. census indicated that about 34,000 Native Americans live in Indiana and Illinois. A thousand years earlier, an estimated 30,000 resided at Cahokia alone. Some experts believe that as many as 75,000 people–a number equal to today's native population in Indiana, Illinois, and Wisconsin–may have called Cahokia home at one time. It is difficult to picture such magnitude, when many other settlements consisted of a few dozen people or a few hundred. Yet, because Cahokia is located at the meeting of the Illinois, Missouri, and Mississippi rivers, with the great Ohio River not too far away, it's possible to justify what is now considered the largest prehistoric site north of Mexico.

Cahokia's focal point must have been the same great earthwork that can be seen today–Monk's Mound, so-called because in the French period, missionary monks found it an ideal spot on which to plant a large vegetable garden. According to analyses, this temple mound underwent more than a dozen stages of development. Today, it occupies 16 acres and stands 100 feet high. Estimates of its inception range from 900 to 1100 A.D. Eighty-five temple and burial mounds remain today in Cahokia, and evidence of the community's size extends for six miles along the banks of the protective waterway.

Cahokia residents lived in houses made of poles and clay, and there is evidence that when one structure burned down, another was built on its foundation. The immediate town was surrounded by a high stockade fence. Outside its gates, the agriculturally-inclined people farmed acres of land, using flint hoes and tools. They planted maize, beans, and squash. Hunters filled their larders with abundant game and fowl, while fishermen reaped the benefits of the many rivers and streams. These rivers and streams also were conduits for trading the crafts produced by the artisans of Cahokia, and for bringing in raw materials for the artisans' use.

The explorations of archaeologists and anthropologists have also yielded what are called "Woodhenges," circles of posts within the area. As is the case with Stonehenge, the "real" purpose of the constructions is unknown, but scientists hazard guesses that the circles were used to indicate planting cycles for farmers. It is also possible that these were Sacred Circles, with the stockaded walls providing some kind of templar protection for priests and shamans as they conducted religious and spiritual celebrations or rituals.

Experts estimate that residents began leaving Cahokia around 1200 A.D. No one knows precisely why, but this is about the time when the Mississippian cultures were being assimilated into the Woodland or Plains

An early mortar and pestle, used to grind grains.

Indian ways of life. There may have been an excessive drain upon the natural resources of the area, due to the large population. An extensive drought might have devastated the agricultural production that sustained the community. An epidemic might have driven people away. No one is certain, because the evidence merely confirms the demise of a cultural location.

It's important to consider, however, the extensive Native American oral histories that provide for the continuum of cultures as they fade away or merge with up-and-coming ones. The Mississippian culture, it should be recalled, survived into the 18th century among Native Americans around Natchez, Mississippi, until they, too, were decimated by explorers carrying French or Spanish flags and traveling up the Mississippi River from the Gulf of Mexico.

Experience with contemporary Native American tribes or nations reveals that much of what is considered conjecture by non-Indian scientists is still believed or practiced in one form or another. If this is put within the context of the Anglo–Saxons, the Normans or the Romans, the Greeks or the Huns, students of culture will find similar retention of antique civilizations in today's Western civilization. The most obvious examples are the various celebrations of the harvest, of the coming of winter, of the emergence of spring.

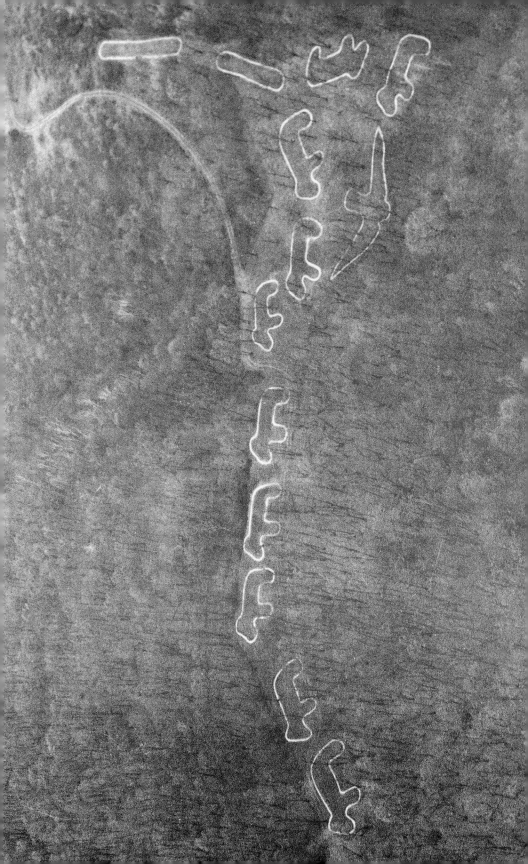

Conclusion

When one considers the variety of civilizations that coexisted with our earliest continental inhabitants several millennia ago, the imagination stretches to include cultures in Asia, Africa, Australia, and Europe. All were different, yet all are similar in many ways. Climate and natural resources were key factors in determining survival and cultural development. While climate dictated the social dimensions of lifestyles and mobility or residence, the utilization of natural resources stimulated science and imagination within the cultures of all continents.

The people who chose the Great Lakes region as their homeland had special talents and specific needs. Their cultures were affected as much by the climate and available resources as by the connection between peoples from other parts of the continent. Though we may try to understand what their lives and their expansive, long-lived cultures meant, we have only semblances of the reality of their total existence. For some travelers, this might seem a tragic loss of contact. For others, it serves as an imperative to open lines of communication with contemporary Native Americans, lines that can provide significant and meaningful connections to those earlier, unwritten epochs.

It's hoped that this guide will sustain those channels of cultural exchange and that, as travelers, we will be wiser for the journey upon which we now embark.

The remarkable Marching Bear Group is the second-largest group of effigy mounds in the U.S., and follows a ridgetop above the Mississippi River.

2
Ohio: Land of Beautiful Rivers

The Buckeye State's name, Ohio, is a French corruption of a Seneca-Iroquoian word for "beautiful river." The state is lined with many beautiful rivers, from the Maumee to the Cuyahoga to the Miami, but its entire southern border is the rambling course of one of the continent's longest, the Ohio River. There is no doubt that the rivers of the area were significant to the earliest transients, and eventually to permanent settlers in the region. The first inhabitants were people designated as Paleo-Indians, who were hunters around 12,000 B.C. and for the next 4,000 years.

While the earliest travelers to Ohio might be visible today only in academic displays of artifacts, there are an appreciable number of remnants of the first Woodland Indians cultures in the Ohio Valley. Today they're called the Hopewell and Adena cultures, because we know them only by the location of their villages, which are marked by elaborate and fabulous mounds. We also call these remarkable people "The Mound Builders."

Mounds

Today travelers can visit places in southern and central Ohio that are considered distinctive and historic: the Miamisburg, Adena, and Serpent mounds for the Adena Culture, and the Seip and Newark sites for Hopewell history. Adena, Miamisburg, and Newark are easy to locate on the map, for these are still populated sites. When one looks for the Seip or Serpent mounds, there is a further need for coordinates, but these too are accessible locations.

In Newark, Ohio, east of Columbus, the traveler will find Adena mounds and the **Mound Builders State Memorial and Museum**. This area contains one of the few Adena villages that has been located. The museum has a Prehistoric Indian Art section, and the historic site depicts "**The Great Circle Earthworks,**" considered a Hopewell creation.

The world's largest serpent effigy mound, however, is readily available to the traveler in the southwestern county of Adams, on Highway 41 and State Highway 73 between Sinking Springs and Peebles. The **Serpent Mound State Memorial**, a raised earthwork constructed to resemble the shape of a snake, extends 1254 feet and ranges in height from four to six feet. The mound is a key to the Adena culture's spiritual personification. In Peebles, there is a **Serpent Mound Museum** that offers a variety of displays of materials belonging to the Adena culture.

A mound at the 2,000-year-old ceremonial site known as Fort Ancient State
Memorial is part of 3 1/2 miles of earth walls.

Twenty miles or so north on Highway 41, the traveler will find the **Seip Mound**, also one of the major reminders of Adena culture. The third significant Adena location in Ohio is near Miamisburg, just outside of Dayton. Here, the **Miamisburg Mound** is situated.

If one is planning a trip and wishes to view the Adena and Hopewell cultures' outstanding mound constructions, Chillicothe is a central point. The traveler can visit the **Adena State Memorial** and the **Hopewell Mound City Group National Monument**, the latter a 67-acre park containing 23 mounds and a museum with an extensive collection of Hopewell artifacts.

While Illinois has Cahokia, the largest ancient site that remains, Ohio has Fort Ancient. Located about 25 miles northeast of Cincinnati off Interstate 71 on State Highway 350, **Fort Ancient State Memorial** is set on the banks of the Little Miami River. An earthwork construction that extends 3.5 miles, Fort Ancient was once thought to be a defensive structure, but archaeologists now suggest that it may be an exceptional, giant calendar.

The **Cincinnati Art Museum** (1720 Gilbert Ave.) is open Tuesday through Saturday, and on Sunday afternoons; there is an admission charge. The museum contains a number of ethnological displays representing Mound Builder cultures, including the Adena, Hopewell, and Fort Ancient peoples. Publications are available. The museum is located fairly near an Adena mound, and some of the displays include materials taken from the site.

The **Cleveland Museum of Natural History** (Wade Oval and University Circle) is open Monday through Saturday, and on Sunday afternoons; there is an admission fee. The museum contains extensive reproductions of early native lifestyles, including burial practices that utilize fiberglass models.

After the Mound Builders

The Temple Mound Builders had vanished by the time European explorers traveled west across the continent. The last surviving group to be defined as such were the Natchez Indians who, by the 18th century, had been decimated by French and Spanish incursions into the Mississippi Delta.

In Ohio from the 17th through the 19th centuries, "temporary" residents of different tribal groups moved inland, away from the expansionist European colonists. Many factors were involved in the migratory or refugee movements. Intertribal alliances were formed to protect, to defend, or to war against other tribal nationalities. The competition between French and English trade companies focused upon maintaining "friendships" with opposing native groups. Epidemics of European diseases forced many tribes to flee homelands in efforts to avoid the plague-like disasters that occurred in their villages.

After the wars of Independence and 1812, the U.S. government began the imperfect system of reservation allocations, continuously changing treaty agreements, altering previously arranged land allotments, and instituting the

Finely shaped examples of spear points.

disruption of tribal societies through outright removal. As a result, for relatively short periods of time, Ohio was considered home by many tribes, including the Mingo, Shawnee, Wyandot, Delaware, Miami, Munsee, Nanticoke, Piscataway-Conoy, Chickasaw, Creek, and Chickamauga-Cherokee. Even the Dakota-Sioux were represented for a time. Depending upon the year, the decade, and the century, there were also Ottawa, Mahican, Tionontati, Ojibwa, Abenaki, Missisauga, and a group called the Moravians, who were comprised of Delaware-Schoenbrunn and Mahican-Gnadenhutten. A Canadian tribe called the Neutrals was also forced south to Ohio during the Iroquois Wars (1641 to 1701).

Little evidence remains of these many settlements and villages, primarily because the locations were subsequently inhabited by westward-moving colonials and then American outposts, forts, towns, and cities. If the traveler seeks the exact locations of places in Ohio that were once inhabited by tribes, perhaps the best reference is **The Atlas of Great Lakes Indian History**, edited by Helen Hornbeck Tanner and published for Chicago's Newberry Library by the University of Oklahoma Press.

Indian wars had their effect upon Ohio Indians, even if they did not occur in the region. The Mesquakie Wars (1719 to 1726), for example, were started

by the Wisconsin-based Mesquakie, aided by neighboring Sauk, Mascouten, Kickapoo, and Dakota warriors, to stop the French and their Indian allies from using Great Lakes routes. In the 1730s, the Wisconsin Ojibwa went against a treaty with the Dakota to clear their old allies from territory in present-day Minnesota and Iowa. This fighting continued well into the 19th century. Meanwhile, Iroquois leaders were selling some of their homelands, occupied by the Delaware and Shawnee, to European newcomers, forcing the "tenants" to go west into Ohio. At about this time, the Huron Wyandots moved to the Sandusky area to build a permanent community. These intertribal affairs began to "frame" resident groups in the Ohio Valley and Lake Erie regions.

The most pivotal event, however, was probably the French and Indian War (1754 to 1760), which pitted the French and British and their respective Indian allies against one another throughout the Great Lakes area. This was followed by Pontiac's War, which began in 1763 in what is now Detroit and extended from the Straits of Mackinac to what is southern Pennsylvania, around Fort Pitt. That anti-British war lasted for at least three years, and what we now call Ohio was very much involved in the conflict.

Tecumseh

One of the greatest orators and leaders of the time was the Shawnee chief Tecumseh (1768 to 1813). Two years before his death, he offered a bleak and poignant commentary on the fate and future of all Native Americans. Here is an excerpt:

What need is there to speak of the past? Where today is the Pequod? Where are the Narragansetts, the Mohawks, the Pocanokets, and many other once powerful tribes of our race? They have vanished before the avarice and oppression of the white men, as snow before a summer sun . . . Look abroad over their once beautiful country, and what see you now? . . . So it will be with your Choctaws and Chickasaws. Soon your mighty forest trees–under the shade of whose wide spreading branches you have played in infancy, sported in boyhood, and now rest your wearied limbs after the fatigue of the chase–will be cut down to fence in the land which the white intruders dare to call their own . . . You cannot remain passive and indifferent to the common danger, and thus escape the common fate . . . You, too, will be driven away from your native land and ancient domains as leaves are driven before the wintry storms.

An actor brings to life the great Shawnee chief, Tecumseh.

Dramas and Events

For the past two decades, travelers to Chillicothe have attended **Tecumseh!**, a presentation called "the spectacular re-enactment of the life and death" of the Shawnee hero. More than one million people have attended the performances at Sugarloaf Mountain Amphitheater, where there is a restaurant, museum, and gift shop. Performances begin in June and end just before Labor Day. For further information, call 614-775-0700, or write to the Ross County-Chillicothe Convention and Visitor Bureau, P.O. Box 353, Chillicothe OH 45601.

Another Shawnee's life has been dramatized, although this individual is an adopted European who eventually became one of the tribe's war chiefs. **Blue Jacket** portrays a man's life, including "friendship with the Black warrior, Caesar, and their struggle to protect the Shawnee homeland against daring frontiersmen such as Daniel Boone and Simon Kenton." This theatrical event is presented from the first week in June through the end of August at the Caesar's Ford Park Amphitheater near Xenia, Ohio, in the Dayton area. You can call the ticket office at 513-376-4318 or the Dayton office at 513-427-0879. A brochure that includes lodging and other area attractions is available from First Frontier, Inc., P.O. Box 312, Xenia OH 45385.

Blue Jacket *cast members hold a council meeting to plan the defense of their homeland.*

The Caesar's Ford amphitheater is also used in late June for a "**Native American Powwow.**" The event is sponsored by the Miami Valley Council for Native Americans. For information, call 513-275-8599. There is also an **Inter-Tribal Arts Experience and Indian Market** held in mid-October at the Hara Arena in Dayton. Native American artists from across the country are invited to exhibit and sell their arts and crafts, including pottery, jewelry, dolls, beadwork, basketry, paintings, sculpture, and textiles. There is also a fashion show and musical entertainment. For further information, call 513-376-4358.

Subscribing to the theory that the Temple Mound Builders' **Fort Ancient** was a kind of calendar, a theory often applied to Stonehenge as well, **SunWatch** is located near Dayton and operated by the Dayton Society of Natural History. Described as a "12th-century Indian village," the living museum recreates the following aspects of village life, according to season: planting, harvesting, house construction, and working artisans. Supervised excavation and various educational classes also take place. During the last weekend in July, there is a special **Summerfest** celebration. For further information contact SunWatch, 2301 West River Road, Dayton OH 45418-2815, or call 513-268-8199.

One of the most unique Native American groups to come to Ohio were the

The "Big House" is the largest structure exposed by excavations at SunWatch. It's interpreted as a council house or headman's residence.

Moravians, a Christian group comprised of the Delaware-Schoenbrunn and the Mahican-Gnadenhutten. **Trumpet in the Land** is a dramatization of the settlement of these two groups in Ohio, following the massacre of nearly 100 Delaware Christians in 1782 at Gnadenhutten. A Moravian missionary, David Zeisberger, was the key mover in an attempt to create a "peaceful Indian settlement along the fiery frontier."

This period of Native American history is among the Ohio region's most fascinating, for it involves the various tribal divisions that evolved during the Revolutionary War. Just as in the French and Indian War, tribal nations took sides. The Delawares were as divided as they had been during the Revolutionary War, and Ohio was one of the vortexes of conflict. The Turtle Clan, for example, was pro-American, while the Wolf were pro-British. The Turkey Clan tried to stay neutral by moving toward what is today Indiana, but eventually returned to join the Moravian converts. The historic George Rogers Clark, brother of famed explorer William Clark, would get involved in the Ohio battle arena, and Daniel Boone would be captured in a 1778 raid by the British-backed Delaware, part of what has come to be called "Dunsmore's War."

Trumpet in the Land dramatizes many of these events, and features a character named Simon Girty, who is described as "a conniving border ruffian." Actually, Girty and his two brothers provide one of the most interesting colonial-Indian connections in American history. Simon and his brothers, James and George, were taken captive years before, during the French and Indian War. Simon was raised by the Seneca of the Iroquois Confederacy, James was brought up by the Shawnee, and George grew up with the Delaware. Each assumed the lifestyle, language, and loyalties of his adopted family, even after the trio was reunited. As a result, George sided with the revolutionary movement, while Simon and James were pro-British. Simon's loyalty to the Crown no doubt explains his latter-day reputation as a "border ruffian."

Trumpet in the Land is "Ohio's longest-running outdoor drama," and it's presented at the Schoenbrunn Amphitheater, located just off Interstate 77 (exit #81) outside New Philadelphia. Nearby places, such as Newcomerstown, Gnadenhutten, Schoenbrunn, and Coshocton have all played significant roles in the Native American history of Ohio. For further information, contact Trumpet in the Land, P.O. Box 450, New Philadelphia, OH 44663, or call the box office at 216-339-1132.

War of 1812 and Post-War Years

Many Americans remember the War of 1812 as the conflict that saw Dolly Madison defending the White House against an alien army while the nation's capitol burned. From history books, some might also recall descriptions of

The infamous massacre of 96 Christian Indians at Gnadenhutten in 1782 is remembered in this scene from Trumpet in the Land.

A dancer at the Indian Summer Festival in Milwaukee.

Commander Perry's defeat of the small British armada on Lake Erie. For Ohio and all points west of the Pennsylvania border, the latter event was more historic than the former, because it meant an end to British attempts to subvert westward expansion by the new American government.

By the 1790s, most of the Native American tribes had been forced to move beyond the Maumee River to Indiana, Illinois, Michigan, and Wisconsin. The U.S. government created a line of strategic forts that signified the outer limits of American "civilization," and most of these were situated in Ohio's Western Reserve and along what would become the Indiana border. This followed the

Fort Harmar Treaty of 1789, which committed the Iroquois Confederacy, the Wyandot and Delaware, plus some Ottawa, Huron, Ojibwa, and Potawatomi, to either stay within prescribed areas or move away.

As soon as the treaty was signed, 52 non-Indian families and 157 "single men" moved into Marietta, Ohio, on the river directly across from Ft. Harmar and founded the "first American town in the Northwest Territory . . . the population center for the Ohio Company," according to one authority. Today, Marietta is a thriving river town on Interstate 77, across the Muskingum River from the site of the old fort, which was named after the general who was ordered to move the Indians from the Ohio region, and was later defeated by them.

There were some Native American tribes who boycotted the treaty sessions and gathered together–with British endorsement–to form the Western Indian Alliance, made up of Miami, Delaware, and Shawnee groups. The Miami were led by Little Turtle, while the Shawnees were captained by Blue Jacket and the Delaware leader was Buckongahelas. The alliance chose to fight the Yankees, setting up a second line of defense near the Ottawa community at the mouth of the Maumee River.

By 1792, following a successful Indian defense of their territory in northern Ohio, the alliance had grown to include a three-man Sioux delegation that had traveled for three months in a single canoe to attend a meeting sponsored by the British. As a result of the meeting, a message was sent to Washington advising the U.S. government to pay poor white settlers to leave the area rather than trying to buy the land from the original residents, who really had nothing in their culture that might be considered "money."

In 1794, however, Major General Anthony Wayne–known as "Big Wind" by his enemies–led a campaign that was won at the Battle of Fallen Timbers. His first act was to build Fort Defiance, and Defiance, Ohio stands on the site today. Wayne subsequently fought his way west, driving the Indians to the mouth of Swan Creek, where Toledo now sits. The battle line continued to move westward, and Wayne ultimately built a fort and named it after himself. Today's community of Fort Wayne, Indiana reflects his vanity. In 1795, the vanquished Indians met at Greenville, Ohio to sign a treaty that ceded two-thirds of the territory. Thus the Wyandot, the Shawnee, the Delaware, the Ojibwa, the Ottawa, the Potawatomi, the Miami, the Wea, the Piankeshaw, the Kickapoo, and the Kaskasia nations gave up rights to Ohio and 16 other strategic tracts of land in the Great Lakes region.

Historical Sites and Organizations

The **Ohio Historical Society** offers a useful booklet detailing more than 60 sanctioned sites and exhibits, a number of which relate to the Native Americans of the region. Among these exhibits are the **Piqua Historical Area**, which is located in a restored homestead and has an "Historic Indian

Ojibwa footwear: The tribe was eventually named after the puckered seams found on their moccasins.

Museum" as part of its displays. You'll find it in Piqua, Ohio; the telephone is 513-773-2522.

Also accessible is **Indian Mill**, located on the Sandusky River and originally a mill built by the government for the local Wyandots. Indian Mill is in Upper Sandusky, Ohio; the telephone is 419-294-3349.

Fort Recovery, in Mercer County, was the site of a significant Indian victory in 1791, while Fallen Timbers, between Maumee and Waterville, was the site where Anthony Wayne defeated an Indian army in 1794.

Western Reserve Historical Society in Cleveland (10825 East Blvd.) is open Tuesday through Friday, and is uniquely designed with the intent of introducing children to Native American history. Eight small dioramas depict

Indian life in various geographic areas, with a special emphasis on life in northern Ohio.

Inscription Rock is located offshore from Sandusky on Kelly's Island. It has an excellent collection of pictographs of human and animal forms, and it's accessible by ferry from Marblehead, Ohio.

In Columbus, the **Ohio Historical Center** has one of the most complete historical, archaeological, and ethnographical collections in the state. The center is located at Interstate 71 and 17th Ave., and the telephone is 614-297-2300. The exhibits range from Paleo-Indian to Fort Ancient and Erie cultures. Dioramas are set up by archaeologists and anthropologists to illustrate what the various cultures were like (or how they are imagined) in Ohio. The center is open daily Monday through Saturday, and afternoons on Sundays and holidays.

Flint Ridge, located near Brownsville, has a museum built over a pit that explains how flint was one of the most valuable resources of the early groups that lived in the area. There are nature trails here, as well.

While some of the state's pre-eminent mounds have been mentioned, there are others set aside as historic sites: **Campbell Mound**, an Adena cone, is south of Columbus; the **Octagon Earthworks** and the **Wright Earthworks** of Newark are both Hopewell constructions. In Circleville, there is the historic **Logan Elm Memorial** where, in 1794, Chief Logan made a memorable speech regarding Indian and non-Indian relations.

In Marietta, there is **Campus Martius: The Museum of the Northwest Territory**, which presents a mainly non-Indian perspective regarding the goals and expectations of the Ohio Company and emerging U.S. frontier policies. The museum is built on the remains of Fort Harmar, and the telephone there is 614-373-3750 or 800-288-2577.

In the same area, near Jackson, there is the **Leo Petroglyph**, containing some outstanding early rock inscriptions and designs. Near Cincinnati and Fort Ancient is **Fort Hill**, a 1200-acre nature preserve that has set aside what might be considered one of the finest early enclosures. Other sites to visit include the **Story Mound** in Chillicothe and the **Williamson Mound** near Cedarville.

Resources

Mound City Group National Monument Library contains 1,500 volumes that deal with the Adena and Hopewell cultures and with other Ohio settlements. The address is 16062 State Route 104, Chillicothe, OH 45601. The library telephone is 614-774-1125.

Rutherford B. Hayes Presidential Center Library in Fremont contains reference materials mainly related to the Plains Indians, but there is also

some information regarding the Wyandot people, as well as records of the Michigan superintendent of Indian affairs (1814-1851); journals of the Rev. J.B. Findlay (there is a Findlay, Ohio), who was a missionary to the Wyandots; and a late 19th-century diary of J.G. Bourke, an "ethologist." The telephone is 419-332-2081.

A number of museums include Native American artifacts, including the **Akron Art Institute**, Coshocton's **Johnson-Humrickhouse Museum**, and the **Cincinnati Art Museum**.

There are four Native American cultural centers in Ohio: Akron's **North American Indian Cultural Center**; the **Cleveland American Indian Center**; the **Native American Indian Center** in Columbus, and in North Olmstead there is the **Ohio Indian Center**.

Native American associations or councils work within the local Indian community and provide the general public with information about various aspects of Native American life. The **Cleveland American Indian Center** (5500 Lorain Avenue, 216-916-3490), for example, offers its membership access to food, health care, and counseling. The center raises funds through several sources, including its **Arts and Crafts Center** in downtown Cleveland (401 Euclid Avenue, 216-781-1447). A center dance group also appears at various public functions. In Youngstown, there is the **Northeastern United States Miami Intertribal Council**. In Dayton, an organization is called the **Shawnee Nation United Remnant Band**.

Cleveland State University (216-231-4600) offers several courses in Native American Studies and provides academic and professional guidance for Native Americans enrolled at the university.

Decorated dance sticks created by the Oneida people.

Native Ohio

△ **Mound Sites**

● **Attractions**

● **Cities & Towns**

3
Indiana: Echoes of History

While the names of several states come directly from the people who were early residents–Illinois and the Dakotas, for example–Indiana was so-called because in the first days of post-colonial settlement, the area was known for its historic ties to Native American peoples. The white authorities who named the territory Latinized the general name for the state's original residents, and created "Indiana." With statehood, the stylized form was extended and the capital was christened "Indianapolis."

Today Indiana remains tied to its historic past. A number of places yet echo with the names, the lives, and the actions of the Kickapoo, Shawnee, Miami, and Potawatomi. There were, however, even earlier residents of what is now Indiana.

Although there's no doubt that Paleo-Indian people hunted and migrated through the region, little evidence exists depicting the lives of these people some 12,000 years ago. Likewise, the "Archaic" peoples unquestionably spent time in present-day Indiana from 5000 B.C. until about 500 B.C. They were hunters and gatherers of the natural resources that the area offered, and there is some scientific evidence indicating that these groups began to domesticate seasonal crops.

Mounds

For about five centuries, the Adena and Hopewell peoples co-existed in the same areas of the Ohio Valley and south of lakes Erie and Ontario. As mound building peoples, their cultures overlap in many ways. The "Hopewell" people built larger mounds and, in some cases, erected their earthworks on top of Adena mounds

In Indiana today there is evidence of considerable mound building, and two primary locations are accessible to the general public. Angel Mounds State Historic Site and Mounds State Park provide the traveler with an opportunity to see how present-day sciences regard the cultures of the Adena and Hopewell peoples.

Mounds State Park (4306 Mounds Road, 317-642-6627), is located about 25 miles northeast of Indianapolis, just off Interstate 69 near the city of Anderson. The park contains ten mounds and earthworks of both the Adena and Hopewell cultures. Chief among them is the "Great Mound," thought to have been built around 160 B.C. The park offers a cultural arts program for

An early 20th century portrait of Wolf Plume, taken by department store photographer Joseph Dixon.

visitors. There are campgrounds, picnic areas, hiking trails, canoe rentals, bridle paths, fishing areas, and cross-country skiing in the winter.

The Temple Mound Builders, also known as the Mississippian culture, basically emerged as the Hopewell people ceased to have an identifiable culture (from 700 to about 1200 A.D.). While the experts are uncertain of the fate of the Hopewell and Adena peoples, there is speculation that war, overpopulation, fragmentation of different subcultures, disease, or assimilation by evolving cultures may explain their apparent disappearance.

One notes that each of the groups–Archaic, Adena, Hopewell, Mississippian–has tended to build upon previous cultures. Archaeologists and anthropologists create cultural classifications, based upon study of the apparently different lifestyles and social systems. However, it should be remembered that their conclusions are based on European methodologies. The scientists have often assumed that Native American cultures have less accurate means of maintaining continuity from one epoch to another, and thus the cultures are considered separate entities.

Those making this assumption may overlook the fact that knowledge among Indian people has been carried forward from a time many centuries before the Vikings, the Irish, or the Italian explorers visited these shores. Many Native American groups are called "The People" in their particular languages, and each has a history that reaches back through time, recalling a continuum of life, spiritual beliefs, cultural practices, and traditions. Indigenous peoples regard their own tribal histories as factual, and may consider the notions of scientists and scholars to be "fantasy histories."

While it is possible to consider the Temple Builders as distinct from their predecessors, such a conclusion is indicative of a fairly narrow analysis. We know more about them simply because they lived during a more recent era. We know, for example, that the Mississippians employed sophisticated farming methods and developed an expanded means of trading goods and resources. Their better-known spiritual practices, especially regarding death and the afterlife, have been the subject of much speculation. Some have assumed that the people who came before the Temple Builders did not have complex spiritual systems, but perhaps it is only the amount of available evidence that differs, not the essential spirituality of native peoples.

Angel Mounds State Historic Site (8215 Pollack Ave., 812-853-3956) is located near Evansville and overlooks the Ohio River, one-half mile off Interstate 164. The mounds are named after the Angels, a family that once owned the land, but the site is now state property. The 500-acre park contains ten mounds constructed by the Temple Mound Builders. It is estimated that as many as 3,000 people once lived in the area. Historians have reconstructed parts of a protective stockade, rebuilt a house, and erected a replicated temple. Each month, lectures are presented on archaeological subjects, ecology, or nature. There is an intepretive center, a library, and a nature preserve on the

This reconstruction from the Mississippian culture can be seen at the Angel Mounds Historic Site.

historic site. A quarterly newsletter called *Smoke Signals* is published, and the museum presents "Ancient Treasure of the Americas: A Pre-Columbian Exhibit." Museum hours are Tuesday through Saturday, 9 a.m. until 5 p.m.; Sunday, 1 p.m. until 5 p.m. There is an admission charge. Each fall, a two-day **Native American Days Festival** is held here, featuring dancers, music, and storytelling.

Sonotabac Prehistoric Indian Mound and Museum (2401 Wabash Ave., 812-885-4330 or 7679) is located near Vincennes. The Sonotabac Mound is considered Indiana's largest ceremonial mound. The museum connected to the site features exhibits that date from 10,000 B.C. to the present day. A monthly newsletter is published by the museum.

Museums

A number of museums in Indiana display artifacts and art objects that reflect the different dimensions of the "pre-contact" Native American cultures.

Indiana University Museum in Bloomington (in the campus's Student Building) has a collection of more than 100,000 archaeological and ethnological specimens having to do with Native Americans in the "New World."

The interpretive center at Angel Mounds.

The **Museum of Indian Heritage** in Indianapolis (500 West Washington St., 317-293-4488) has a large Native American collection that includes archaeological and ethnological materials, although the major emphasis is on Northeast Woodland, Great Plains, and Southwest cultures. The museum publishes a quarterly newsletter.

The **Children's Museum of Indianapolis** (3010 North Meridian St.) is open Tuesday through Saturday and Sunday afternoons. Its exhibits include dioramas that deal with early native daily life.

Northern Indiana Historical Society Museum in South Bend (112 South Lafayette Blvd.) offers exhibits of "prehistoric" Native Americans, as well as the mound building cultures. There is a lifestyle exhibit based on the more contemporary Potawatomi and Miami nations' existence in northern Indiana. A quarterly newslettter is published, entitled *The Old Courthouse News.*

The **Glenn A. Black Laboratory of Archaeology** (9th and Fess, 812-855-9544) in Bloomington is a research facility devoted to Native American archaeology, but its field museum showcases Great Lakes and Ohio Valley archaeology and Native American cultures. The hours: Monday through Friday, 8 a.m. until 5 p.m.; Saturday and Sunday, 1 p.m. until 4:30 p.m.

Allen County Fort Wayne Historical Museum in Fort Wayne (302 East Berry St., 219-426-2882) is located in the old city hall. It contains an exhibit titled "Ft. Wayne's History from the Ice Age to the Space Age." Hours are

Tuesday through Friday, 9 a.m. until 5 p.m.; Saturday and Sunday, noon to 5 p.m. There is an admission charge.

Indiana Historical Society in Indianapolis (315 West Ohio St., 317-232-1882) was founded in 1830. It contains a public collection and a research library, and the Society publishes books on Indiana history. Open Monday through Friday, 8 a.m. until 4:30 p.m.; Saturday from 8:30 a.m. to 4:30 p.m.

In Indianapolis there is the **Museum of Indian Heritage** (6040 DeLong Rd. in Eagle Creek Park), which presents exhibits devoted to the range of Native American habitation in Indiana.

Indiana State Museum in Indianapolis (202 North Alabama, 317-232-1637) has an "exploration of Hoosier history from the Ice Age" onward. Hours are Monday through Saturday, 9 a.m. until 4:45 p.m.; Sunday, noon until 4:45 p.m.

Wabash County Historical Museum in Wabash (State Route 13 and Hill St., 219-563-0661) has what is described as "a magnificent artifact collection."

"Post-Contact" in Indiana

About 50 years after Plymouth Rock, a French expedition first entered what is now northern Indiana. The French found the place inhabited by one of

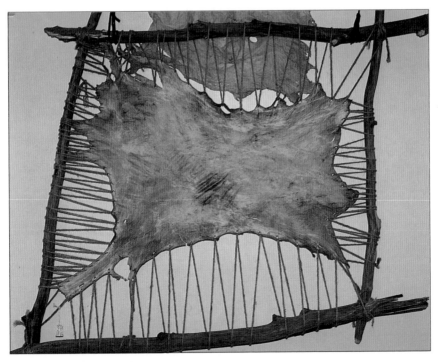

A hide-stretching framework used by the Oneida.

the Algonquian Confederacy groups, the Miami. Over the next 100 years, the Potawatomi would settle the area, extending into what is now southern Michigan as well as parts of Illinois and Ohio. The Kickapoo, another of the Algonquian groups, would also lay claim to some territory in Indiana.

"Miami" is a fairly common place name in North America, from Florida to Oregon. There are rivers in Ohio called the Big Miami and the Little Miami. In Native American Indiana, however, it is thought that "Miami" is derived from an Algonquian word for "people of the peninsula," primarily meaning the current Michigan's lower half. The Miamis of Indiana, Michigan, and Ohio were hunters, chasing down buffalo, for example, on foot, or enclosing them in a circle of fire with everyone in the group taking part in the hunt.

Many aspects of the hunting and fighting traditions of the Plains Indians emanated, it is thought, from people like the Miami, who were eventually forced to emigrate beyond the Mississippi. The traditions range from the use of pipes in diplomatic situations, celebrations, or declarations of war to the recounting of heroic deeds in battle.

There were many colonial clashes during the time between the landing of the Pilgrims and the American Revolutionary War. The first came between the French and the English, who fought over trade routes and relations with various Native American nations. On several occasions, the two European powers pitted their Native American allies in battles against one another. The Mesquakie Wars (1719 to 1726), for example, were begun by a small tribe in Wisconsin that persuaded the Kickapoo, Sauk, Mascouten, and some Dakota people to try to stop French traders from using Great Lakes routes. And in the early 1730s, the Ojibwa of Wisconsin turned against their Dakota allies in Minnesota and tried to push the Dakota out of their lands. Both conflicts were encouraged or inspired by Europeans.

In the middle of the 18th century, the Iroquois Confederacy was selling off some of its land holdings to European settlers and trading companies, thereby forcing the Delaware and Shawnee further west. The Huron Wyandots moved from Canada to the area near present-day Sandusky, Ohio, and into parts of northeastern Indiana. This began the most radical era of westward migration for major Native American nations, and Indiana would become one of the primary routes of passage.

The French and Indian Wars (1754 to 1760) most directly pitted the Native Americans against each other as they sided with British or French expansionist efforts. The Algonquians and other tribes agreed to help the French, while the Iroquois supported the British. This meant that one group was often pitted against another in cruel battles where the European forces were, at best, rag-tag militia or frontiersmen.

A young dancer at Milwaukee's Indian Summer Festival

The Native Americans of Indiana were generally uninvolved in the fighting. But scarcely more than a dozen years after these wars ended, many tribes were asked, expected, or commanded to take sides in the American Revolutionary War.

Tippecanoe and Tecumseh

With the establishment of the Northwest Territory, the native peoples of Indiana were very much involved in conflicts related to settlement, emigration, and compulsory relocation. The great chief of the Shawnee, Tecumseh, played a decisive and historic role in his opposition to these developments. He was also part of the tragic circumstances that created a slice of American history remembered as "Tippecanoe and Tyler Too."

The Tippecanoe River flows through the center of Indiana. Tecumseh and his brother, Tenskwatawa, also known as "The Prophet," moved from Ohio to the Indiana Territory to create, at the confluence of the Tippecanoe and Wabash rivers, what they called "Prophets Town." Tecumseh was known throughout the Native American nations and the United States as a supreme peacemaker and a relentless campaigner for Indian unity.

Prophets Town, located near present-day Lafayette, was to be a community that would recognize and foster the universal values of all tribes and nations. Indians of many nations came to settle in the town, as Tecumseh promised them a life free of non-Indian influences and pressures.

Shortly after he and his brother and their followers built the first longhouses, Tecumseh embarked on an international mission of persuasion.

He travelled west, north, south, and east, talking with tribal leaders about Indian unity and military alliances against all outside powers. While Tecumseh was away from Prophets Town, Indiana Territorial Governor William Henry Harrison began playing havoc with Indian nations in the area. He invited a group of sub-chiefs, who had no authority to negotiate, to sign the Treaty of Fort Wayne (1809), which ceded three million acres of land to the government. The Native Americans were provided an allotment of $7,000.

Upon his return, Tecumseh ruled the treaty null and void, and found 1,000 warriors willing to back him in his resolve. For two years a tenuous peace prevailed between the two sides, but in 1811 Governor Harrison demanded that some Potawatomi men who had allegedly killed settlers in Illinois be turned over to his court of justice. Tecumseh refused.

In what might have been his only political or military blunder, Tecumseh then departed on another mission of unification. The mission was not inappropriate, but the great orator's timing proved unfortunate. As soon as Tecumseh was away, Harrison gathered a rough militia of 1,100 men, some from as far away as Virginia, to march upon Prophets Town.

Although Tecumseh had always counselled for peace and moderation,

A contemporary actor portrays the great orator, Tecumseh.

Tenskwatawa learned of the force marching against the community and, encouraged by a militant group of Winnebagos in Prophets Town, went out to oppose the enemy.

Three miles outside of the village, he and his warriors attacked the sleeping militia. They won the first skirmish, but realized that they must retreat and

Lookout Mounds site

establish a unified front. They returned to Prophets Town, gathered their families and their possessions, and headed westward. When Harrison and his army marched into Prophets Town on the Tippecanoe River the next day, it was deserted. His army burned the community to the ground on that day in November of 1811.

The War of 1812 began soon afterward. Tecumseh's dream of united Indian nations and joint military alliances died. The groups from Prophets Town went back to their peoples and, as the British declared war on the Americans, the Indian nations began to join the conflict. Tecumseh responded to a British call for military aid from Native Americans in the Northwest Territory. He was given some assurance that, if victorious, he would have the opportunity to establish a special Indian Territory, to be known as Indian Country.

Showing their confidence in his leadership, the British made Tecumseh a brigadier general. He led joint forces successfully against Fort Detroit and Fort Dearborn (later the site of Chicago). He even went head-to-head against his old enemy Harrison at Fort Meigs on the Maumee River in Ohio. The war's tide turned, however, with the death of the British general who was his military mentor, and with the victory of Commodore Perry over the British navy on Lake Erie. The English began a retreat to Canada, and Tecumseh's multi-national Native American army was ordered to provide defensive cover. On October 5, 1813, Brigadier General Tecumseh was killed in battle. He was 45 years old.

Tippecanoe Revisited

Tippecanoe Battlefield National Historic Landmark is located at Battleground, Indiana (317-567-2147). The landmark offers interpretation of "10,000 years of Indian occupation, battles, and presidential campaigns centering around Tippecanoe." The landmark is open from March to November, 10 a.m. until 5 p.m.; and from December to February, 10 a.m. until 4 p.m. There is an admission charge.

The Battle of Tippecanoe is a drama performed in West Lafayette (4450 State Route 43 North, 317-463-1811). The drama illustrates "a conflict of cultures, rather than right versus wrong." Performance dates begin in the second week of June, and the seasonal curtain falls during the last week of August. Performance times: Tuesday through Sunday, 8 p.m. The box office is open Tuesday through Sunday, 1 p.m. until 9 p.m. Tickets are required.

The **Wabash Heritage Trail** of the Tippecanoe County park system in West Lafayette (317-423-9363) is a 13-mile hiking trail from the Tippecanoe Battlefield Park to the site of Fort Ouiatenon. The fort was captured by Indian forces during Pontiac's Rebellion in 1783. The trail is open from dawn to dusk "in dry weather."

The March Westward

In 1816, the non-Indian population of Indiana stood at an estimated 350,000. By 1830 that number had greatly increased, and the Native American

The "Great Mound" near Anderson, Indiana

population had decreased to fewer than 5,000 people. The Potawatomi maintained 36 communities in Indiana, totaling about 2,500 citizens, while 23 Miami villages held a combined residency of about 1,000. Only a few Kickapoo and Ottawa were left. The Shawnee had been forced beyond the Mississippi River. The Delaware were gone from the White River around Muncie and Anderson, and the Wea were forced from their land by an 1820 treaty.

The Miami, whose holdings were solely within the boundary of the state of Indiana, chose to split their nation, with half of the members moving west and the others staying. The ones who remained became homeowners, farmers, and livestock raisers, and many were quite successful within the American system of enterprise and capitalism. In fact, when Miami Chief Jean Baptiste Richardville died in 1841, he was regarded as Indiana's wealthiest man.

Many Potawatomi fought against the ceding of their land to the incoming population. In 1836, a number voiced their unhappiness to the government, but they did not succeed in their oppposition. Their land lay directly in the path of a planned east-west road that would extend from Detroit to Chicago. With the opening of the Erie Canal in 1825, the land became critical to the expansion of the U.S. midwest. By 1840, the reluctant Potawatomi were gathered for a forced march to Kansas–one that had tragic results. Many people died in transit.

Currently, numerous land claims are being argued by Native American nations, and many of these include territory in Indiana. The groups involved include the Miami, Potawatomi, Wea, Delaware, Piankeshaw, and Kickapoo. Their claims are based on treaties signed individually or collectively between 1804 and 1827.

Museums

One of the more remarkable figures involved in Native "Americana" is Joseph Dixon, a sometime minister and public relations agent for the Wanamaker (New York) department stores in the early years of the 20th century. At one time, Wanamaker felt the American people needed to see the "majesty" of the nation's first citizens and, in fact, the retailer hoped to build a rival to the Statue of Liberty. The statue, in the form of a giant Indian, would welcome immigrants to American shores. Dixon was sent on a mission that lasted more than a decade, taking photographs of Native Americans from coast to coast.

Two of Dixon's Wanamaker collections are found in Bloomington. The **Indiana University Museum** houses 15,000 of these photographs, and an 8,000-image collection is kept at the **William Hammond Mathers Museum** (601 East 8th St., 812-855-6873).

The bronze deer sculpture at the entrance to the Eiteljorg Museum of American Indian Art.

Items from "Spirited Hands:Continuing Traditions in Native American Art," a permanent exhibit at the Eiteljorg Museum.

Elsewhere, the **Potawatomi Museum** in Fremont (North Wayne and city limits) has 5,000 "historic and prehistoric" items, as well as a library.

The **Eiteljorg Museum of American Indian and Western Art** in Indianapolis (500 W. Washington St., 812-636-9378) proclaims that "the West begins at the Eiteljorg." The museum's collection includes Native American art and artifacts. Open Tuesday through Saturday. 10 a.m. to 5 p.m.; Sundays from noon to 5 p.m. There is an admission charge.

The **Ashby House** in Ladoga (County Road 350 East, 317-567-2147) is a restored 1883 home, and among its collections is a Hopi exhibit. Admission is by permission only, and there is a fee charged.

The **Pendleton Historical Museum** in Pendleton (317-778-4248) is set at Fall Creek, site of "The Fall Creek Massacre", which was actually a minor skirmish between settlers and Indians. The museum is open May through October, Saturday and Sunday from 1 p.m. until 5 p.m.

The **Miami County Museum** in Peru (51 North Broadway, 317-473-9183) contains a collection of local history that ranges from Miami cultural artifacts to Cole Porter. It's open Tuesday through Saturday, 10 a.m. to 5 p.m. There is an admission charge.

Sites and Parks

Pigeon Roost State Historic Site in Scottsburg (U.S. 31 seven miles south of Scottsburg, 812-265-3526) has a 40-foot monument that "pays homage to 24 settlers who lost their lives in an Indian raid in 1812."

Ouabache Trails Park in Vincennes (Rural Route 6, Fort Knox Road, 812-882-4316) is a 254-acre park with campgrounds (open April to October) that has historical connections to Tecumseh, William Henry Harrison, and Zachary Taylor. The park itself is open year-round.

The **Old Iron Bridge** in Warsaw (121 North Indiana St., 219-269-1078) crosses the Tippecanoe River and was originally built on the township line that separated the Chief Mota and Chief Checosee reservations.

For further information regarding parks, sites and museums, contact the **Indiana Tourism Department** (1-800-289-6646 or 317-232-8860), or the **Division of State Parks**, Indiana Department of Natural Resources. The address for the latter is 402 West Washington St., Room 298, Indianapolis IN 46204. Telephone: 1-800-622-4931.

Petroglyphs at Roche-a-Cri State Park

A male dancer's bustle, created by the Oneida.

Publications

In addition to the museum and library publications noted above, there is **Indian Progress**, published in Frankton by the Associated Executive Committee of Friends of Indian Affairs, a missionary project of the Religious Society of Friends (Quakers). The publication began in 1869, and its work is concentrated on Indian Centers in Oklahoma and Alabama. *Indian Progress* is published three times a year. The address is 612 Plum St., Box 161, Frankton, IN 46044. Telephone: 317-754-7977.

College Courses

Ball State University in Muncie (317-285-1575) offers a minor in Native American Studies through the anthropology department. Its special curriculum is the "Interdisciplinary Native American Studies Program."

Purdue University in West Lafayette (317-494-4672) offers a number of courses through the departments of sociology and anthropology. These include "Indians of North America," "Indians of the Greater Southwest and Great Basin," "The Archaeology of North America," "Native American Religious and World Views," and "Peoples of Middle America."

A collection of spear points and arrowheads from the Aztalan site.

Native Indiana

4

Illinois: Home of the People

"Illinois" is a French interpretation of the term the Woodland Indians used to describe themselves when the two groups first met in the 1670s. In the tribal language, the term meant "The People." Although the Illinois nation was a relatively small one, it became the namesake of a river, then a territory, and in 1818, a state.

Mounds

In the reference volume *The World of the American Indian*, a map indicates the extent of mound building in the U.S. Illinois is notable because of the concentration of mounds "in uncounted thousands" that follow the Mississippi, Illinois, Wabash, and Ohio rivers. Central Illinois, south and east of the Illinois River, however, is a vacant space on the map.

Archaeological maps in *The Atlas of Great Lakes Indian History* reveal that there are only five major sites in Illinois. The Huber-Berrien site is located in the Chicago-Gary area, at the confluence of the Illinois and Mackinaw rivers. Vincennes is situated on the Illinois-Indiana border, where the Wabash River separates the two states. These sites are considered Upper Mississippian and Woodland cultures.

The oldest sites of archaeological exploration in Illinois are at the southeastern and southwestern corners of the state. One, known as "Caborn," is connected to the Angel Mounds site in Indiana, and is situated at the junction of the Wabash and Ohio rivers. The second is located at the intersection of the Missouri and Mississippi rivers, and it's referred to as "Cahokia." Another site is known as "Sand Prairie." At Caborn and Sand Prairie, little is left other than collections of artifacts. The Cahokia site, however, is most remarkable.

Cahokia Mounds State Historic Site near Collinsville (7850 Collinsville Rd., 618-346-5160) reveals much about what was once a thriving community through its interpretive reconstructions, its well-tended, isolated mounds, and its museum and educational center. The museum has more than 30 exhibits, ranging from displays to dioramas and exterior reconstructions, including "Woodhenge." The educational center offers Native American craft classes, a lecture series, a slide and tape presentation about Cahokia, and a newsletter. There is also a research library. In late September, **Heritage America** is held here, an event where "all North American Indian cultures will converge on Cahokia Mounds." See chapter one for a description of life at Cahokia.

An aerial view of the Twin Mounds at Cahokia.

Museums and Institutions

Two exemplary collections of materials regarding Native American history and heritage are housed in Chicago.

The **Field Museum** (Roosevelt Road at Lake Shore Drive, 312-922-9410) is a nine-acre institution with more than 15 million artifacts and specimens of scientific and historical interest. It includes seven exhibit halls devoted entirely to Native Americana, and special exhibits are periodically presented. The museum publishes *The Field Museum Bulletin* as well as catalogs, handbooks, and leaflets. An admission fee is charged.

The **Newberry Library** (30 West Wilson, 312-943-9090) is a unique American library, utilized primarily for studious research and investigation. In total, the library houses more than five million manuscripts and books, as well as 60,000 maps. Key to the library's collection of Native Americana is the extensive **D'Arcy McNickle Center for the History of the American Indian**. Within this endowed section of the library is much information relating to Native Americans, from the earliest times forward. For example, there is the E.E. Ayer Collection, which consists of thousands of volumes, manuscripts, prints, and photographs. Parts of the D'Arcy McNickle Center are devoted to American Indian and non-Indian contacts, Native American linguistics, government relations, and a broad range of maps. The center publishes a newsletter entitled *Meeting Ground.*

The Newberry Library also sponsors the **American Society for Ethnohistory** (60 West Walton, 312-975-7237), which conducts research in areas of global ethnicity, including Native American and Alaskan cultures. The

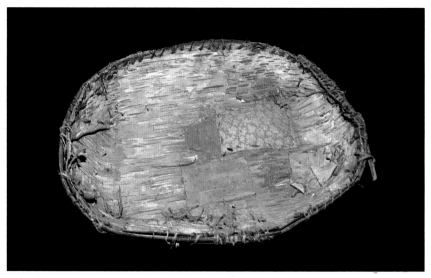

A basket constructed of birch bark.

library publishes books such as *The Atlas of Great Lakes Indian History* as well as other publications, and maintains a comprehensive bookstore.

Dickson Mounds Museum in Lewistown (Route 1, 309-547-3721) is considered an on-site facility, and the mound is unique because it is housed within the museum. Archaeologists continue to exhume and examine the remains of 234 people buried between 1150 A.D. and 1350 A.D. in the Mississippian culture earthwork memorial. Because the museum directly exposes skeletons that were placed in a sacred manner, the museum and the dig are protested by state, regional, and national Native American groups. Legal actions are pending at this writing.

It should be noted that these protests are not registered solely on the grounds of secular disrespect for hallowed ground and those buried within. For many Native Americans, burial is the means of spiritual reunification with essential elements of life. When a gravesite is entered, it is believed that spirits not meant to be released will be set free, thus disturbing the basic balance of the natural order. While it may be difficult for non-Indian scientists to appreciate the concern over intrusions, many in Native American and non-Indian cultures find these acts to represent the highest sacrilege.

The **Illinois State University Museum** in Normal (301 South Main St., 309-438-8800) provides a general focus on the cultural heritage of Illinois, including changing exhibits on history and anthropology. The museum's permanent repository includes a "Dickson Mounds skeletal collection," so this aspect of the museum's exhibit is challenged and opposed by Native American groups.

The **Paublo Agricultural Museum** (217-692-2858) is midway between Blue Mound and Stonington, and exhibits "the story of agriculture, from past to present." This includes the Native American experience with domestic agriculture, which goes back more than 2,000 years.

The **World Heritage Museum** in Urbana (484 Lincoln Hall, 702 South Wright St., 217-333-2360) contains "The Story of Mankind," an exhibit that covers our habitation from the cave to outer space.

The **Crawford County Historical Museum** in Robinson (Lincoln Train College, 618-544-3436) offers an extensive archaeological display of artifacts collected in Crawford County that reflect life since prehistoric times.

Illinois State Historical Society in Springfield (Old State Capitol, 217-782-4836) is dedicated to the collection, preservation, and dissemination of Illinois history. It consists of 160,000 volumes and six million documents, including materials about the state's early residents.

One of the most enigmatic of the state's historical sites is located north of Alton, high on a Mississippi River bluff. It is called the **Piasa Bird** (Route 100, 618-465-6676), and it's the replication of "a pictograph discovered by Fr. Marquette in 1673 and described in his diary." The resulting re-creation very much resembles the griffin, a mythical European creature with wings and a

A "story stone" containing a fox carving, found near Aztalan.

reptilian tail. This one, though, is without the usual lion's head. Instead, its head appears bearded and topped with deer's antlers.

The **Kampsville Archaeological Museum** in Kampsville (618-653-4316) is part of the Kampsville Archaeological Center, and it relates the early history of the Illinois area through artifacts and photographs provided by the center's students over the years. Events are held at the center and museum each summer. An example is "The Making and Breaking of a Prehistoric Pot," which revealed the life of a piece of pottery from its creation and decoration to its fate in the ground and its "discovery" through modern archaeology. In early August, the center also holds an annual **Archaeology Day**, with site tours, experiences in "primitive technology," and presentations on the methods used to identify artifacts.

Woodland Days

The days of the Woodland Indians in Illinois were relatively open and free in pre-contact times, most likely due to a sparse population. Most of the tribal settlements were seasonal communities for Native Americans living in the Ohio Valley, Michigan's lower peninsula, and Wisconsin, as well as those from the Missouri-Mississippi confluence. Nearly all the people living in what is now Illinois were of Algonquian heritage, with some Siouan people along the northern and western borders.

The wars between Indian nations swirled all around Illinois, but for the most part stayed outside of this particular region. Fighting that pitted the

Ojibwa and Nipissing against the Dakota and Mesquakie took place west and south of Lake Superior. The Iroquois Wars (1641 to 1701) mostly stretched north to Green Bay and south to Shawnee territory at the Ohio-Indiana border, although in the 1680s groups from the New York and Canadian Iroquois Confederacy made incursions into Illinois.

The French Connection

The involvement of "local" tribes in conflicts seems to coincide with the entry of the French into Illinois. There were three primary battle sites in the area. The first was located at the convergence of the Vermillion and Illinois rivers, where battles between 1682 and 1700 involved the Miami, Illinois, and Shawnee tribes. The major battle here was fought in 1684 at the French outpost, Fort St. Louis.

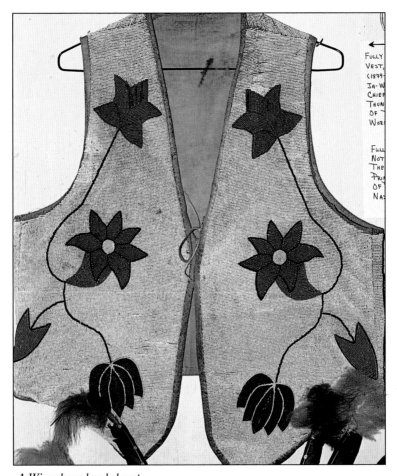

A Winnebago beaded vest.

Another significant battle was fought south of Fort Chicago in 1687, where the Iroquois massacred a group of Miami. And the earliest battle took place in 1680 near the ruins of Cahokia, where the Illinois River joins the Mississippi. Here the Iroquois defeated the Tamaroa, and additional conflicts were waged between the Illinois, Ottawa, and Tionontati tribes.

The 1684 battle took place at what is now called Starved Rock, as the Iroquois failed in an attempt to take Fort St. Louis. According to legend, Starved Rock is named after a band of Illinois that retreated in a battle against another tribe. The Illinois warriors selected a high sandstone butte as their last position of defense. As the story goes, the band members decided to starve rather surrendering to their enemies.

Starved Rock State Park near Utica and Peru (Route 178, 815-667-4906) today retains much of the natural beauty and resources that made it desirable for settlement over the centuries. The park's 2,630 acres include 18 canyons, a dozen waterfalls, and 125-foot-high bluffs, all of which encourage hiking, camping, canoeing, and horseback riding.

The park's grand lodge and conference center was built by the Civilian Conservation Corps in the 1930s, and its museum (815-667-4726) is devoted to the history of the park and the region.

The French connection was made in the 1670s, when the famed French missionary-explorers Louis Joliet and Jacques Marquette traveled down the Mississippi. A Jesuit priest named Father Claude Jean Allouez spent several years living with the Illinois tribe, and was no doubt instrumental in securing an alliance between the Illinois and the French military in 1680, under the command of Rene Robert de la Salle. For the French, the Mississippi was the primary conduit south to the trade and political power base they had established in Louisiana.

For nearly a century, the Illinois-French compact held war away from the Illinois people, even though they maintained their traditional enmity with the Algonquians of the Great Lakes and the Sioux to the north and west. The major problems for the Illinois–a nation made up of several bands including the Cahokia, Kaskaskia, Michigamea, Moingwena, Peoria, and Tamaroa–arose when the French were fighting the British for territorial political control and trade routes in the Great Lakes basin.

At one point during Pontiac's Rebellion in 1763, as the great Ottawa chief was successfully fighting the British, the Illinois became allies of one of their longtime enemies–no doubt persuaded by the French to forget their hard feelings toward the Ottawa leader. However, when an Illinois assassinated Pontiac in 1769, allegedly hired by the British to do so, the Illinois band suddenly faced an array of hostile tribes. The Ottawas rallied the Ojibwa, Potawatomi, Sac, Fox, and Kickapoo nations to avenge the death of their leader.

Starved Rock, named after an Illinois band that refused to surrender.

The Illinois was never a large tribe. Rather, it was a composite of several relatively small bands of extended families. It's thought that by the time the Ottawa alliance had achieved its revenge, a vengeance unstoppable due to sheer numbers, the population of the Illinois had gone from perhaps 2,000 to under 200 people. These beleaguered survivors, mostly from the Kaskaskia and Peoria bands, found their way to the French settlement of Kaskaskia, on the Kaskaskia and Mississippi rivers.

The Illinois stayed out of harm's way until 1833, when they sold their small land holdings and moved to Kansas, joining with two Miami bands–the Wea and Piankashaw–that had moved out of Indiana. The entire group journeyed to northeastern Oklahoma, to an area then known as Indian Territory, where descendants of the tribe that gave the "Land of Lincoln" its name still live today.

Museums

The French influence was of great significance to many Native Americans who called the Illinois region home at one time or another, and vestiges of that influence remain. In Romeoville, for example, there is the **Isle a la Cache Museum** (501 East Romeo Road, 815-886-1467), located on a historically strategic island in the Des Plaines River. The museum is dedicated to portraying the fur trade between the French and their Native American partners.

In Evanston, there is the **Mitchell Indian Museum** (2408 Orrington Ave., 708-866-1395), located on the campus of Kendall College. The museum presents Native American artifacts and crafts including tools, weaponry, beadwork, basketry, pottery, carvings, and jewelry. There is also an exhibit of Navajo rugs. The museum is open daily except during college holidays and the month of August.

The **Letourneau Home Museum** in Bourbonnnais (Stratford Drive and Route 102, 815-933-2535) is a refurbished 150-year-old mansion built by the founder of the city. Its exhibits contain artifacts taken from archaeological digs on the surrounding property.

The **Burpee Museum of Natural History** in Rockford (813 North Main St., 815-965-3132) contains a broad range of natural history exhibits, including a Woodland Indian display.

The **Funk Rock and Mineral Museum** in Shirley (Route 1, 309-827-6792) exhibits the rocks and minerals collected by seed corn magnate LaFayette Funk II, including Native American artifacts.

The **Illinois State Museum of Springfield** (Spring and State Sts., 217-782-7386) has a number of "lifelike" re-creations of Illinois' Native American villages and lifestyles.

In Carthage, the **Kibbe Museum** (118 North Scofield St., 217-357-2119) displays two centuries of Hancock County history, including Native American residency, as well as Mormon and Civil War history–the Mormon leader Joseph Smith was lynched in Carthage.

Fort Crevecoeur Park, in Creve Coeur between Pekin and East Peoria (301 Lawnridge Drive, 309-694-3193), is the site of the first French fort in Illinois. The **Annual Crevecoeur Rendezvous** (309-674-9192), held in late September, re-enacts French and Indian relations from around the year 1675.

The **Geneseo Historical Museum** (216 South State St., 309-944-3043) has the "largest arrowhead and Indian exhibits in Illinois." There is an admission charge.

The **Massac Historical Museum** in Metropolis (4th and Market Sts., 800-248-4373 or 618-524-5120) exhibits the French and Indian connection, and is located in a refurbished home that was built in 1870. **Fort Massac State Park**, also in Metropolis (1308 East 5th St., 618-524-4712) contains a reconstructed pioneer fort and features hiking trails, picnicking, boating on the Ohio River, camping for a fee, and a museum.

Kickapoo Resistance

When the Illinois were driven from their northern territory, the Kickapoo took control. They divided into two groups, one of which left for the prairies to hunt buffalo on the far side of the Mississippi. The other group settled where the Vermillion and the Illinois rivers meet, also the site of the French outpost, Fort St. Louis. When the two bands separated, they became what anthropologists call the "Prairie Algonquian" and the "Woodland Algonquian."

The Vermillion band fought against the intrusion of non-Indian settlers, joining in both Little Turtle's War (1790 to 1794) and Tecumseh's Rebellion (1812 to 1813). These direct Indian-U.S. confrontations were among the first of the armed conflicts that arose as western migration of European-American settlers increased. A number of tribal leaders fought small holding actions that stopped the flow momentarily, but these ultimately had little effect on the westward tide. The Illinois area became the final stand for the Kickapoo and the Sauk nations east of the Mississippi.

The Kickapoo Resistance was caused by two bands, one headed by Mecina and the other by Kennekuk. Mecina used military techniques including sabotage and night-raiding to frighten off incoming non-Indians. However, he was soon overwhelmed by the number of settlers, and was forced across the Mississippi into Missouri, then Kansas, then into Indian Territory.

Kennekuk fought more of a "mental battle" against the settlers, employing a passive resistance that kept the government of Illinois and the federal government shuffling papers and ideas for more than a decade. His method was to come up with valid reasons for not moving, ranging from starvation to illnesses to evil omens. It worked until 1832, when suddenly northern Illinois was filled with soldiers–not looking for Kennekuk, but not exactly willing to ask whether the Indians they encountered were Kickapoo or Sauk.

Kennekuk was in fact among those who aided the valiant, against-all-odds cause of the Sauks, but when that conflict ended, he realized that the

Kickapoos had to leave. Their history and heritage did not end, however, when they left Illinois. They followed the route of Mecina's band, but when they arrived in Indian Territory they once again split into two groups. Some crossed Texas and moved into Mexico, becoming a militant Kickapoo band that fought against both sides of the U.S. Civil War when threatened–and against the Texas Rangers as well. Although many of these were eventually repatriated to Oklahoma after the U.S. Cavalry seized their women and children as hostages, a number of Kickapoo still live in Mexico today. The nation still lives in Kansas, Oklahoma, and Mexico, and its citizens have maintained their special heritage, beliefs, and arts and crafts.

The Black Hawk War

Native Americans fought many wars against various immigrant forces, among them intruding tribes. The conflicts included King William's War; Queen Ann's War; King George's War, which began in the Caribbean in 1739 as the War of Jenkin's Ear; the Great War for Empire; and the French and Indian War. In Europe, parallel struggles took place–the War of Grand Alliance, the War of Spanish Succession, the War of Austrian Succession, and the Seven Years' War. All had their impact on European-Native American relations.

Tribal alliances with European powers also stimulated Indian-Indian wars, including the Tuscarora War, the Yamasee War, the Cherokee War, the Natchez Revolt, the Chickasaw Resistance, and the Fox Resistance. In many cases, the Native Americans were valuable military pawns moved from one battle to another. Many times they fought traditional enemies, but on some occasions they were mercenaries, fighting alongside those same enemies. In many cases, European military victories were dependent upon the fighting abilities of tribes or tribal mercenaries. But tragically, no matter which side they fought on, whether in victory or defeat, the Native Americans always lost something. Usually, they lost their traditional territories.

What evolved into the Black Hawk War of 1832 was triggered by "reneging" on an 1804 St. Louis treaty that had tricked some Sauk and Fox into ceding their Illinois holdings to the U.S. government. As was the case in Indiana, the government's chief negotiator had been William "Tippecanoe" Henry Harrison.

As Tecumseh had done in Indiana, the Sauk leader repudiated a treaty that was negotiated under false pretenses and chicanery. The leader was Makataimeshekiakiak, or Black Sparrow Hawk, later known as Black Hawk. He and his band came from Saukenuk, now Rock Island, where the Rock and Mississippi rivers meet. They refused to cede their land, and rebelled against the treaty for more than a quarter-century. The Sauk fought brief skirmishes in 1808 and 1811, and sided with Tecumseh in the War of 1812. Black Hawk

Sculptor Lorado Taft's tribute to Black Hawk.

even led an attack against the Wisconsin Territory's Fort Howard after the war had officially ended.

"My reason teaches me," Black Hawk wrote later, "that land cannot be sold. The Great Spirit gave it to His children to live on. So long as they occupy it and cultivate it, they have a right to the soil. Nothing can be sold but such things as can be carried away."

Today the Quad-Cities of Davenport, Rock Island, Moline, and Bettendorf stand where Black Hawk and his band cultivated the soil. When Illinois became the 21st state in 1818, calls increased for the enforcement of Harrison's treaty. Once, when Black Hawk and his band went on winter hunt, non-Indian squatters settled into his warm-weather lodges.

Black Hawk and his people returned to Saukenuk in the spring, and the squatters chose to summer elsewhere. However, a chief named Keokuk persuaded a number of Sauk and Fox to move across the river to Iowa. Black Hawk refused, for it was the traditional planting season. He and his people coplanted with area settlers, and the groups coexisted peacefully after some hard words were initially exchanged. With the harvest, Black Hawk promised to return again in the spring.

In 1827, President Jackson announced that all Indians would be relocated west of the Mississippi. At about this time, a considerable amount of lead was being mined in the Galena area, north of Saukenuk, and settlers didn't feel secure with a Native American band in the area that still traveled to Canada to talk to the British in Ontario.

This time, winter provided Illinois Governor John Reynolds with the chance to force the Sauk out of Saukenuk forever. He rallied the Illinois militia and the U.S. Army, a force including people who would become significant in American history 30 years later: Col. Zachary Taylor, Lt. Jefferson Davis, Capt. Abraham Lincoln, and Daniel Boone's son, Nathaniel. When they arrived at Saukenuk, they found the village deserted. Black Hawk had taken his people across the Mississippi, but returned under a flag of truce. He persuaded military negotiators that he might leave the area peacefully.

The U.S. and Illinois forces left, believing they had avoided war. But Black Hawk was buying time, waiting to be joined by his allies, the Fox, and by a Winnebago prophet named White Cloud, who had enlisted warriors from the Winnebago, the Potawatomi, and the Kickapoo. Altogether, Black Hawk mustered a force of more than 500 men who promised to follow him to Saukenuk so that he and his band could plant their crops in spring.

The two opposing forces reached the Rock River on April 12, 1832. One month later, Black Hawk sent a peace party under a white flag, but the militia fired on the group, killing three Indians. After the American attack, Black Hawk led an expeditionary force of just 40 Indians forward, driving the 275-man

A beautiful example of Winnebago basketry.

American force into a chaotic, 25-mile retreat. The retreat was led by Major Isaiah Stillman, and the military reaction became known as "Stillman's Run."

After Stillman's Run, Black Hawk feared retaliation. He and his relatively small band disengaged themselves from their allies and fled north into Wisconsin Territory. Meanwhile, the alliance began attacking non-Indian settlements and miners. In response, President Jackson sent Gen. Winfield Scott to Illinois. Scott stopped in Chicago to rally a militia, which would include men from Wisconsin. The new army was hit by an epidemic of cholera even before it left Chicago. The Wisconsin forces, under the leadership of territorial militia commander Henry Atkinson, were bogged down in the Rock River swamps and marshes as Black Hawk and his people escaped westward.

The speed of Black Hawk's movement west reduced the size of his group to his own Sauk band, including women and children. They hardscrabbled their way north, crossing what is now the campus of the University of Wisconsin in Madison, pursued by Atkinson's militia. When the militia was joined by the remnants of Scott's force, a pincers was created that channelled the Sauk band toward the Mississippi. A fierce fight took place on the shores of the Wisconsin River, which Black Hawk had hoped to use as his avenue to the Mississippi.

Many Indians died in the fighting along the waterway. He and his people crossed land to the Bad Axe River, but they were by now a very small band short of food, energy, and reserves. Black Hawk tried to negotiate when they reached the Mississippi in July, but his diplomats were fired upon by soldiers from the shore. The women, children, and old people trying desperately to paddle canoes or swim across the Mississippi were also shot at. Sharpshooters found the situation not unlike shooting fish in a barrel. More than 300 Sauk people died on that day.

If anything was then certain beyond the tragedy of the moment, it was the fact that the Mississippi River would be, for a while, the boundary of peaceful relations between Native Americans and the United States. Black Hawk and the Winnebago prophet White Cloud were among the few to escape the fusillade. However, later in the same month, they surrendered in the Winnebago territory of Wisconsin.

"Farewell, my nation," the Sauk chieftain said in his speech of capitulation. "Black Hawk tried to save you, to avenge our wrongs. He took the blood of some of the whites. He has been taken prisoner, and his plans are stopped. He can do no more. He is near his end. His sun is setting, and he will rise no more."

Black Hawk's release was negotiated on the condition that he would relinquish his rank as chief. He was taken to meet Andrew Jackson, the engineer of the fundamental policy that would serve to remove and defeat Indian nations for a century to come. He was paraded in the East, and he died an embittered man. Even after he was buried by his people, his grave was robbed and his head was displayed in a traveling carnival exhibit.

Meanwhile, Keokuk moved his Sauk people to Iowa, where they sold their lands, then on to Kansas and finally to Indian Territory in what is now Oklahoma. Some Sauk returned to Iowa and bought back territory, so small reservations or trust lands remain in the three states, but there are no Sauk or Fox in Illinois or Wisconsin.

It should be noted that perhaps the most renowned Native American of all time, at least to non-Indians, was a Sauk. Bright Path was born in 1888. He was sent to the Carlisle Indian School in Pennsylvania, the first off-reservation school sponsored by the federal government. At the school he was registered as Jim Thorpe, and he became one of the greatest athletes of his (or any) era.

Memorials

Stillman's Run Memorial Park in Stillman Valley (Route 72, 815-645-2603) reflects the May 14, 1832 battle. The dozen Illinois militiamen who fell in the first fight with Black Hawk are buried at the site.

In Rock Island, the **Black Hawk State Historic Site** (1510 46th Ave., Route 5, 309-788-0177) is considered one of the largest Indian centers in North America, and is dedicated to Black Hawk's "vain attempt to regain (a) homeland."

In the Rock River Valley's **Lowden State Park** (815-964-6482), the traveler will find noted Illinois sculptor Lorado Taft's largest work, a fifty-foot statue of Black Hawk.

In Galena, the **Old Stockade Refuge** (208 Perry Street, 815-777-1646/0352), is the last remaining structure standing from the Black Hawk War. It was used as a shelter by frightened settlers as the conflict raged through the area. Today there is a Native American museum within the site, and there is an admission charge.

History and Heritage

The **Chicago Historical Society** (Clark St. and North Ave., 312-642-4600) has collections and exhibits relating to the early settlement and history of the Chicago area.

The **Freeport Art Museum** (121 North Harlem Ave., 815-235-9755) displays examples of Western and Asian art, including Native American works.

The **Museum of Natural History** in Urbana (1301 West Green St., 217-333-2517) contains numerous anthropological displays, including Native American exhibits that emphasize the Illinois bands, the Navajo, the Pueblo, and the aboriginal residents of Greenland.

The **Western Museum** in Macomb (Western Illinois University, 300 Sherman Hall, 309-298-1727) has Native American clothing and artifacts among

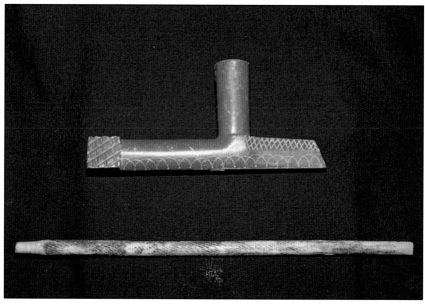

A ceremonial pipe, which might have been used in diplomatic situations, in celebrations, or in declaring war.

a variety of historic displays.

The **Hauberg Indian Museum** in Rock Island (1510 46th Ave., Route 5, 309-788-9536/0177) is part of a historic site, and the museum "depicts the daily lives and seasonal activities of the Sauk and the Fox through artifacts and life-sized dioramas" from around 1800, including bark-covered summer and winter homes. Other displays involve artifacts of the Eastern Woodland Indians, and tribes of the Plains, the Northwest, West, and Southwest. The museum has published *Two Nations, One Land: A Cultural Summation of the Sauk and Mesquakie (Fox) in Illinois.*

The **Madison County Historical Society and Museum** in Edwardsville (715 North Main St., 618-656-7562) has a "grand collection of Indian artifacts," primarily John R. Sutter's 3000-item collection, which includes artifacts from the Southwestern nations.

The **Trail of Tears Campsite** in Jonesboro (Route 146, 618-833-4910) is considered "a memorial to an American tragedy." Specifically, the site is where the southern Cherokee stopped during their tragic, two-year forced march to Oklahoma. There is an admission fee to the campsite.

The **School of Nations Museum** in Elsah is part of Principia College (618-374-2131), and it offers a collection of Native American crafts including dolls and textiles, as well as a library.

Events and Festivals

During the last weekend of May, an **Indian Powwow** is held near Areola at the Rockome Gardens (217-268-4106). In addition to dancing, there are crafts for sale and stories to be told.

Custer's Last Stand Festival of the Arts (708-328-2204) takes place in Evanston during the last week of June. The festival is headquartered on Custer Avenue, and it involves several blocks of displays by artists and crafts people, as well as "Native American artists' powwows."

Moweaqua Powwow Days (217-768-4717) in July may or may not include Native American participation on an official basis, but is a four-day sequence of cultural events and activities.

In Belleville, the **American Indian Celebration** (9500 West Illinois, Route 15, 618-397-6700) is held at 7 p.m. at the National Shrine of Our Lady of Snows. As part of the mid-July celebration, the area's Native American community holds the annual **Feast of Kateri Tekawitha**, in honor of a woman who may become the first Native American saint in the U.S. Following the formal ceremony, Native American dancers provide their gift of traditional dancing.

In Kankakee, there is **A Gathering on LaSalle's Theatiki–An Historical Re-enactment** (815-933-9905), which dramatizes the heritage of the French and Indians in the area before 1830. The event is held in mid-July.

In mid-August, Shelbyville hosts the **Okaw Indian Festival** (Visitors Center, Lake Shelbyville, 217-774-3951), where "an early American heritage exhibit" features Native American crafts and lore.

The **American Indian Center** (312-275-5871) in Chicago sponsors three powwows. In May, over the Mother's Day weekend, the **Spring Arts and Crafts Exposition and Powwow** is held at St. Gregory's Catholic Church. In late June, the annual summer **American Indian Center Powwow** takes place at the Lake County Fairgrounds. And for the past four decades, another powwow has been held in late fall. The weekend-long event includes over 300 dancers, singers, and drummers.

Associations and Organizations

The **American Indian Library Association** is affiliated with the American Library Association (50 East Huron Street, Chicago, 312-944-6780). Its mission is to promote the development, maintenance, and improvement of libraries, library services, and information services on reservations and within the communities of Native Americans and Native Alaskans. The AILA also publishes the *American Indian Libraries Newsletter*.

The American Academy of Pediatrics has a **Committee on Indian Health** located in Elk Grove (P.O. Box 927, 1141 NW Point Rd., 312-228-5005).

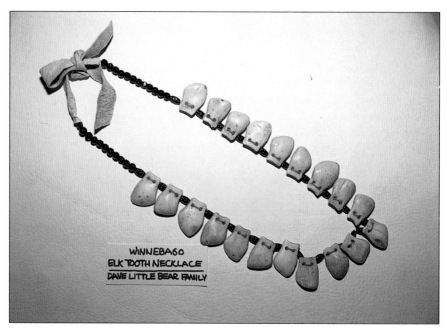

A necklace created from elk teeth

Founded in 1965, the committee is dedicated to improvement of pediatric services to Native Americans and Native Alaskans through the Division of Indian Health of the U.S. Public Health Service.

In Chicago, there is also the **American Indian Health Service** (838 West Irving Park Road, 312-883-9100); and the **Native American Committee** (4546 North Hermitage, 312-728-1477), which publishes *Redletter/ANA*.

The **Commission for Multicultural Ministries** of the Evangelical Lutheran Church in America, located in Chicago (8765 West Higgins Rd., 312-380-2700), consists of a nine-member board of Native Americans and Native Alaskans who act as advocates to the Lutheran Church on behalf of native interests and rights.

Study Programs

One of the more unique educational institutions in the country is headquartered in Chicago. The **Native American Educational Services (NAES) College** (2838 West Peterson Ave., 312-761-5000) offers an accredited program, sanctioned by the Commission on Institutions of Higher Education of the North Central Association of Colleges and Schools. A Bachelor of Arts degree in community studies is offered to people employed in American Indian programs in four communities–Chicago, Minneapolis-St. Paul, the Fort Peck Reservation in Montana, and the Menominee Reservation in Wisconsin. NAES College also offers a special Tribal Languages Studies curriculum. The college has a library with archives and research resources. A biennial college catalog is published, and the institution has published *Annotated Bibliography of the Chicago Indian Community, 1893-1988* and *Indians in the Chicago Area.* NAES College prints a newsletter called *Inter-Com* and a quarterly entitled *NAES Rule.*

The University of Chicago includes an **Institute of Indian Studies** (Foster Hall, 312-702-8638).

Native American Centers

Chicago's **American Indian Center** (1630 West Wilson, 312-275-5871) publishes a periodical called *The Warrior.*

St. Augustine's Center in Chicago (4512 North Sheridan Rd., 312-784-1050) works with the city's Native American community.

Two pipes–one used by a man, the other by a woman. The woman's pipe contains a deer etching.

1 .... Black Hawk State Historic Site
2 .... Burpee Museum of Natural History
3 .... Cahokia Mounds State Historic Site
4 .... Chicago Field Museum
5 .... Chicago Historical Society
6 .... Crawford County Historical Museum
7 .... Dickson Mounds Museum
8 .... Ft. Creve Coeur Park
9 .... Ft. Massac State Park
10 .... Freeport Art Museum
11 .... Funk Rock and Mineral Museum
12 .... Geneseo Historical Museum
13 .... Hauberg Indian Museum
14 .... Illinois State Historical Society
15 .... Illinois State University Museum (Normal)
16 .... Illinois State Museum of Springfield
17 .... Isle A La Cache Museum
18 .... Kampsville Archaeological Museum
19 .... Kibbe Museum
20 .... Letourneau Home Museum
21 .... Lowden State Park
22 .... Madison County Historical Society & Museum
23 .... Massac Historical Museum
24 .... Mitchell Indian Museum
25 .... Museum of Natural History (Urbana)
26 .... Old Stockade Refuge
27 .... Paublo Agricultural Museum
28 .... Piasa Bird Historical Site
29 .... School of Nations Museum
30 .... Spoon River
31 .... Stillman's Run Memorial Park
32 .... Trail of Tears Campsite
33 .... Western Museum
34 .... World Heritage Museum
35 .... Starved Rock State Park

Native Illinois

△ Mound Sites

● Attractions

● Cities & Towns

5
Michigan: Big Lake Territory

In the Ojibwa-Algonquian language, Michigan means "big lake." When we look at the map of Michigan we realize how appropriate the name has become, for the state today is framed by the lakes of Superior, Huron, Erie, and Michigan–all but one of the Great Lakes. Here also are two key waterways, the Sault Ste. Marie and the Detroit River.

When the great Wisconsin Glacier covered the northland, both Michigan and the Great Lakes were crushed beneath a two-mile layer of ice and snow. Until about 10,000 years ago, therefore, the area was not habitable, and so the people of the time made their way to warmer, more hospitable climes.

Needless to say, there is very little evidence of Paleo and Archaic Indians in Michigan. Even the Adena culture stayed away. Some petroglyphs have been found, such as the Sanilac Petroglyphs near Grand Rapids in the southern part of the state. For many centuries, however, the area was simply too cold and too wet. Later, as the Hopewell culture and the Mississippian-Temple Mound Builders broadened their horizons, Michigan became a remote outpost of some significance.

A significant number of mound sites have been documented in Michigan over the years. The sites are not heavily clustered, as they are in Ohio or along the Mississippi, but a fair distribution exists in the eastern part of the lower peninsula–especially along the shoreline of Lake Huron and the Detroit River. The upper peninsula appears to contain only a half-dozen locations along the Keweenaw Bay peninsula.

Ancient Times

Evidence of early residence can be found in only a few places today, but some Michigan museums and historical societies have interesting collections. **Teysen's Woodland Indian Museum** in Mackinaw City (416 North Huron St., 616-436-7011) includes a collection of artifacts dating back to 10,000 B.C. The museum is open from May through October.

At Port Austin in the Port Crescent State Park (Germania Road, 517-738-8663) are the **Sanilac Petroglyphs**, a series of fascinating images carved into sandstone outcroppings.

Michigan State University in East Lansing (101 Museum, 517-355-2370) holds what has been termed an exceptional collection of Upper Mississippian Mound Builders' pottery, works that are smooth-surfaced and globular, with

The former site of Father Marquette's mission is now a museum displaying Ojibwa culture.

Teysen's Woodland Indian Museum: The bear serves as the museum's "logo."

rims that turn up and outward. Many have excised decorations and were tempered with crushed shells. The museum contains exhibits dedicated to other Native American arts and artifacts, as well as those centering around Great Lakes archaeology.

In Grand Rapids, the **Public Museum** (54 Jefferson, 616-456-3977) has a collection of Hopewell artifacts. The only public display of the Temple Mound Builders is in Grand Rapids as well, at what are called the **Norton Mounds**.

The Council of Three

Three of the major Algonquian peoples were known as the "Council of Three Tribes." The council included the Ottawa, a name that means "to trade"; the Potawatomi, which means "people of the place of fire" or "keepers of the sacred flame"; and the Ojibwa, named after their distinctive style of sewing a puckered seam on their moccasins. Later, the Ojibwa name would be mispronounced by the French, and "Chippewa" would be the result. The three tribes collectively called themselves the *Anishinabe*, i.e. "the Human Beings" or "the First People."

The Anishinabe first resided along the St. Lawrence River many centuries ago, and their migration to the upper Great Lakes took hundreds of years. Lake Superior, called *Gitchi Gamig*, became their final destination, and was considered a sacred body of water.

According to Anishinabe history, the three tribes traveled for 500 years from the site where "The Great Miracle," or *Gitchi Manito*, had created them. The people had been given the Megis Shell, a kind of seashell that brought them together and indicated where they should go. The image of this shell appeared five times during their migration west. When, at last, they reached *Gitchi Gamig*, each tribe went a different direction. The Ojibwa headed from the mouth of the St. Lawrence River to what is now Chequamegon Bay and Madeline Island, part of northern Wisconsin. The Ottawa settled in the area where the Straits of Mackinac and the Sault Ste. Marie divide the three great lakes. The Potawatomi chose the southern half of the lower peninsula.

The Council of Three Tribes maintained a close relationship and shared heritage throughout the intense years when rival nations, mostly Britain and France, would fight for territory and trade that the Anishinabe had maintained for hundreds of years. That struggle began with the Iroquois Wars (1641 to 1701), thought by many to have been inspired by the British as a means of pushing the French out of Canada.

In 1655 and 1662, there were two significant battles at the Sault St. Marie. In the earlier conflict, the Ojibwa and the Ottawa fought and defeated the eastern Iroquois. Seven years later the Ojibwa again battled for the same territory and won. In that year, 1662, there was also a pitched fight for the island of

An ornate birchbark bowl displayed at Teysen's Museum.

Michilimackinac, and here the Ottawa kept the Iroquois from taking the strategic island in the straits between the upper and lower peninsulas.

Perhaps even more significant than these and the other battles with the Iroquois, who were conducting an aggressive war of expansion west, was an incident at the Sault in 1671. At that time, the French announced that the interior of North America, from the headwaters of the Mississippi north and west to the Mississippi River delta, was now part of New France. Spain, meanwhile, claimed the territory west of the Mississippi.

Here's one account of this notable pronouncement: "Accompanied by music and medieval pagaentry, [the French emmisary] addressed fourteen groups of Indian people living south, west, and north of Lake Superior. The ceremony took place at the Jesuit mission of Saint Marie." On this day the French wanted furs, trade routes, and copper, but they also wanted souls.

The role of the Sault in the early European history of North America is a pivotal one. The Jesuits who built the mission had plans as ambitious as those envisioned by the fur traders and copper miners. Within two decades, they had established missions on the territories of 18 different tribes. In almost all cases, a fort was built near the Jesuit mission.

One of the key events–socially, politically, commercially, and religiously–was the annual summer gathering of Native Americans at Michilimackinac. The French sponsored the event and, in the period between 1671 and 1691, thousands made the pilgrimage each year. The Jesuit mission at St. Ignace organized the event so that the tribes could peacefully carry on serious trade negotiations and come to agreements. The event became a kind of United Nations conclave, or perhaps was an early equivalent of meetings of the European Economic Community.

Each summer meeting provided non-Indians, religious or sectarian, with an opportunity to gather information about the lifestyles, the cultures, the languages, and the concerns of Native Americans. At these great gatherings, the roots of ethnological study were planted, and these roots would provide the European community with basic and often erroneous information about the initial inhabitants of this continent.

Museums

Several museums provide insight into this exciting and relatively peaceful interaction between two different world views. At St. Ignace a museum has been built on the site of **Fort de Baude** (334 North State St., 906-643-8686), which was built by the French in 1681. The museum contains displays and exhibits of the Woodland Indian cultures that lived in or visited the area.

A panther effigy mound, built to resemble the animal.

A Winnebago-crafted basket.

Also in St. Ignace is the **Marquette Mission Park and Museum of Ojibwa Culture** (500 North State St., 906-643-9161), which is on the site of Fr. Marquette's mission. The 19th-century building here houses a number of displays of Ojibwa culture, and is open from Memorial Day through September.

On Mackinac Island, there is the state park's museum, which has a collection of Great Lakes Indian materials, as well as a display of historic Ojibwa apparel. The island also has an **Indian Dormitory**, where visitors to the Indian Agency often stayed.

The **Marquette City Historical Society Museum** (213 North Front St., 906-226-3571) has an extensive collection of Native American archaeological materials from the upper peninsula, particularly the Ojibwa culture. The dioramas and tribal scenes include examples of basketry, tools, medicinal materials, textiles, canoes, and other aspects of daily life. The Marquette museum also publishes a quarterly magazine, and has printed books entitled *Indians of Gitche Gumee* and *Harlow's Wooden Man*.

Cadillac to Pontiac

As the Iroquois Wars wound down, the French had plans of their own, one of which was to foreshadow later attempts to bring several Native American nations together in a kind of communal coalition. In 1701, the year marking the end of the Iroquois imperial dream, the French built Fort Pontchartrain on the Detroit River's northern point. The founder was Antoine de la Mothe Cadillac, who had served for eight years at Fort de Baude. Cadillac persuaded the Huron and Ottawa to come south from the Straits, and the Potawatomi and Miami to come from the St. Joseph River at the base of Lake Michigan. He was successful in getting Ojibwa, Sauk, and Mascouten to come from around Green Bay.

Cadillac's goal was to bring 6,000 Native Americans to the Detroit area, but it was not an idea whose time had arrived. It might have been workable if the invited nations were related and friendly, but the French encouraged mutual enemies to come to Detroit. Inevitably, in 1706, the Ottawa attacked the Miami, and the French had to take sides with their allies, the Ottawa. Five years later, the Mesquakie moved in on Huron and Ottawa territory with only massacre in mind. The Fox Wars began, and within a year there were only Huron and Potawatomi on the Detroit side of the river, while the Ottawa had moved east to what is now Ontario.

The Mesquakie did not like the French, partly because the French government imposed a 20-year ban on fur imports (due to a glutted market) after the Mesquakie struck a fur trade agreement. The government action had an impact on all Indian nations dealing with the French, but it particularly incensed the Wisconsin Mesquakie. They hated the Illinois, who were longtime French allies, and persuaded the Sauk, the Mascouten, the Kickapoo and some Dakota/Sioux to harass the Illinois, an action that continued from 1719 to 1726.

During this period, the French were stymied by a blockade along the Fox River and Mississippi River trade route, which connected the entire Great Lakes trade route to New Orleans and France. The French even built Fort Beauharnois in an effort to break the Dakota/Mesquakie alliance, but the tactic didn't work. The Mesquakie were soon attacking the Illinois once again. Finally, in 1727, the French convinced their anti-Mesquakie allies to push the Mesquakie south. The effort was relentless, and within six years only 50 Mesquakie remained alive. They joined the Sauk, whom the French also drove south as far as the Rock River. A century later, this Sauk terrain would become Black Hawk's rallying point.

At the time of the Seven Years War in Europe (1756 to 1763), some startling changes were happening on the "New World" side of the Atlantic. The French had long felt pressure from the British, and the two powers had previously fought in several locations for territorial supremacy. Today, these are viewed as the French and Indian Wars, beginning in 1689 with King William's War. But it was the Great War for Empire (1754 to 1763) that resolved the supremacy question—for a few years, that is.

The term "French and Indian" more or less indicates that the British were the undeclared enemy. More accurately, France's Indian allies were pitted against England's Indian allies, with the European powers providing war materials and certain strategies. The majority of the combatants were Native

Americans fighting traditional enemies for payment of one sort or another, rather than for glory, territory, or heritage. The ultimate goal of both European powers was control over territory already held by Indian nations.

One sad historical accident foreshadowed future, intentional actions against the Indians. Charles Michel de Mouet, whose father was French and whose mother was Ottawa, became a very successful leader of combined forces during these wars. As a commander, he led his army against several key British forts, including Fort Duquesne and Fort Pickawillany in the 1750s. When he and his forces defeated Ft. William Henry, his medical personnel apparently did not realize that some of his wounded Menominee and Potawatomi Indians from Michigan's St. Joseph River area were taken into the fort's hospital ward, where smallpox patients had been treated. When these veterans returned home, their communities were decimated by the fatal disease. Years later, many tribes were given blankets by traders and the military that once covered diseased and dying people, with similar–and intentional–results.

The most prominent British defeat of the French came in 1761 at Michilimackinac. Soon they circled the lakes, taking one French fort after another. Fort St. Joseph, on the St. Clair River, and Fort Detroit were among the first to fall in 1760. Ft. Detroit would fall into and out of French and British hands for several decades.

One of the great moments in the conflict occurred in 1763, when Ottawa Chief Pontiac began his own rebellion against the British invaders. Pontiac had considered the British an enemy for years and had fought against them many times, but this time, inspired by a Delaware spiritual leader known as the Delaware Prophet, Pontiac rallied to a cause. The Delaware Prophet advocated a return to the Indian way of life, including the disposal of firearms. Pontiac agreed with the first tenet, but he realized that firepower was the key to many military victories. He also favored maintaining his nation's longtime relations with the French.

Needless to say, the French backed the latter concept, and agreed to help him return Fort Detroit to its rightful owner. Pontiac tried to take the fort by subterfuge, sending a team of peace negotiators inside, armed under their blankets and robes. However, when Pontiac saw that the odds were against him, he told the multi-tribal council that the time was not right for capturing the place. So he and a number of other tribes beseiged the fort, setting in motion a number of attacks on non-Indian settlements in the area. An estimated 2,000 settlers died in the spring and summer of 1763.

Meanwhile, the Potawatomi were taking back the fort located in their territory, in what is now Niles. And following Pontiac's orders, the Ottawa, Miami, Kickapoo, Wea, and Wyandot tribes took forts in their areas, as far west as Green Bay and east to Pennsylvania. The cleverest victory took place at

An artist tried to imagine how Chief Pontiac might have looked, and produced the drawing at left.

A copper trader's pot, which might have been traded for furs in the 17th century.

Michilimackinac on June 2, 1763. The Ojibwa and Sauk were "entertaining" the British with a game of lacrosse. An Ojibwa misplayed the ball and sent it inside the fort, signaling the takeover. He and his teammates rushed inside after the ball, then captured the garrison. The only problem arising from the capture was the fact that the Ottawa were upset because they weren't part of the game plan.

The Pontiac Rebellion ended with the Treaty of Paris in 1763, whether the Ottawa alliance liked it or not. Pontiac never took Fort Detroit, and with the European treaty he lifted the seige. The Proclamation of 1763 stated that there would be no further non-Indian expansion across the continent, but of course that clause was dramatically ignored. Pontiac was assassinated in 1769.

Museums and Centers

The **Genessee Indian Center** in Flint (124 West First St., 313-239-6621) has a "living museum" portraying Great Lakes Indian cultures through demonstrations of different lifestyles in special settings.

Lansing's **Michigan Historical Museum** (505 North Washington Ave.) is the historical division of the Michigan Department of State, and it offers numerous exhibits of Native American history related to the development of Michigan.

In Detroit there is the **Fort Wayne Military Museum** (6325 W. Jefferson,

313-297-9360) and the **Detroit Children's Museum** (67 East Kirby). The latter is sponsored by the public school system and contains a special collection of Native American crafts and arts, including basketry, musical instruments, textiles, pottery, and tools. The Children's Museum also has a library with a number of Native American materials.

In Ann Arbor, the **University of Michigan Exhibit Museum** (1109 Geddes Ave., 313-764-0485) has "extensive holdings of Native American archaeology and anthropology," including the Hinsdale Collection of Great Lakes basketry, as well as exhibits and collections from other Native American and Native Alaskan cultures.

In Niles, the **Fort St. Joseph Museum** (508 East Main St., 616-683-4702) has a collection of Woodland Indian artifacts, as well as the Plym-Quimby Collection, which deals with Sioux materials including drawings by Sitting Bull. There is also a library within the museum.

Bay City's **Historical Museum** (321 Washington Ave., 517-893-5733) presents Native American and fur trading history in three-dimensional interpretive exhibits.

Near Buchanan, **Bear Cave** (4085 Bear Cave Rd., 616-695-3050) evidences traces of Potawatomi occupation, and the cave was later used by the Underground Railroad as a hiding place for escaped slaves.

A luminescent example of a box made with birchbark and quills.

In Copper Harbor, there are two sites with Native American connections: the **Astor House Museum** (Minnetonka Resort, 916-289-4449) and the **Delaware Copper Mine** (P.O. Box 148, Kearsarge, 906-289-4688). The nearby Brockway Mountain Drive is called "the highest above-sea-level drive between the Alleghenies and the Rockies . . . the most scenic drive in the Midwest."

In Midland, the **Chippewa Nature Center** (400 South Badour Rd., 517-631-0830) is an educational, non-profit institution that includes two museums with Native American displays. The center also offers 12 miles of trails.

In Sault Ste. Marie, there is the **John Johnston House Museum** (400 Hudson Drive, 906-632-6255), built after the Revolutionary War. Johnston was a noted fur trader in the north country, and married the daughter of famed Ojibwa chief Waubojeeg. Later the couple's daughter would marry Henry Schoolcraft, the first federally-assigned Indian agent.

In Tawas City, the **Tawas Historical Indian Museum** (1702 South U.S. 23, 517-362-5885) offers a display of North American Indian artifacts, as well as prehistoric tools. The museum is open from April through November.

Post-Revolution

After the American Revolution, there were numerous incursions into Michigan Territory. The British had largely lost their influence, but they hung on to Detroit despite the terms of the second Treaty of Paris of 1783. Detroit would remain a pivotal spot for another three decades, but the general expansionist movement of Americans westward would largely bypass Michigan for the broader expanses of Indiana and Illinois. In 1805, Ohio housed about 250,000 non-Indians, while Michigan had only 4,800.

The area belonged largely to the Ojibwa, the Ottawa, and the Potawatomi, with part of the upper peninsula occupied by the Menominee. The War of 1812 brought the fighting back home, however. For the first year of the war, the British maintained a war zone on both sides of the Detroit River, rallying several former French allies to fight the Americans. The forces recaptured Fort Mackinac, and attacked ferry and supply boats as well as traders. All around Detroit–at Grosse Isle, Brownstone Creek, Swan Creek, Raisin River, Put-in Bay, and around the Sault at Detour Point–there was fighting. Hostile Potawatomi moved to take the fort at St. Joseph River.

The major Native American figure in this new drama was the great Shawnee chief and orator Tecumseh who, with his twin brother, the Prophet, had already suffered the frustration of dealing with territorial governor William Henry Harrison for several years. The British called upon Tecumseh's ability to rally allies and made him an official general in the British army. One of of the first tasks was defending Detroit; Tecumseh and his multi-national army routed U.S. General William Hull's forces. For a time, the British-Indian

The Marquette Mission Park offers "living history" exhibits.

alliance ranged far and wide across the Northwest Territory, from Iowa to Ohio, causing the surrender of several opposing forces, including the Kentucky troops of U.S. General James Winchester in 1813.

Then Tecumseh's nemesis, General Harrison, moved in and agressively pushed north toward Detroit. Harrison's concern was the overland route between Detroit and St. Joseph and then on to Chicago, which is basically followed by today's U.S. Highway 12.

The British rallied their own forces. The Potawatomi established a "secret" town south of what is now Kalamazoo. Menominee, Ojibwa, Ottawa and Winnebago came south from Mackinac, along with the now-friendly Dakota,

Oneida instruments: a water drum with a bear carving, and a horn rattle.

Mesquakie, and Sauk, led north by Chief Black Hawk. The British thought that 3,000 warriors and 900 English soldiers could handle anything the Americans threw at them, but Harrison landed 5,000 soldiers and militia where they were not expected, and the route was on. In the ensuing battles, Tecumseh was killed. The war in the west was fundamentally finished, especially with Commander Perry's naval victory on Lake Erie.

Although there were several suspicious meetings between notably anti-American tribes on the British side of the Sault Ste. Marie, not much resulted. One meeting in 1816 included representatives of Black Hawk and the Santee Sioux Little Crow (see the Minnesota Uprising), but it was also known that the Menominee and the Winnebago were unhappy with British interference in their trading routes.

In 1822, the Americans built a fort at Sault Ste. Marie as a military and political gesture indicating the value that the U.S. placed on this land. Henry Schoolcraft was appointed the first U.S. agent to the Indians. Although he was initially a geologist whose strength lay in locating mine sites, during more than two decades of residence in the area, Schoolcraft would become the country's first genuine ethnologist. He married the granddaughter of a great Ojibwa leader, and his notebooks and journals are yet being rediscovered by Ojibwa and non-Indian alike as meaningful documents of a culture that was intact 170 years ago.

There were numerous Ojibwa, Ottawa, and Potawatomi villages in Michigan Territory in 1830–two dozen in the upper peninsula and more than 130 in the lower peninsula. Many of those communities bear the same names today, such as Manistee and Muskegon. In the Grand Valley, Ottawa maintained 2,500 acres of corn and raised apples on orchards containing 3,000 trees. Potawatomi and Ottawa lived in the Kalamazoo River Valley, while the Saginaw River Valley was Ojibwa territory.

The small town called Lyons, situated on the Maple River between St. Johns and Ionia, was once named Coocoosh after a highly respected leader of the Ojibwa and Ottawa, Muckatycoocoosh. That name was given to him as a black infant, when he was taken in an 1812 raid. In the 1830s, this black man became regarded by his tribal kinsmen as a major spokesman.

Other names were changed as settlers moved in. Kiskkawkaw became Bay City; Arbetchewachewan was changed to Midland; Shinwakoosing was rechristened St. Louis; and Otusson became Frankenmuth. But in 1830, the land northwest of Saginaw was almost totally uninhabited by non-Indians, and those to the south depended upon the Native Americans for vegetables, fruits, game, and medicinal treatments.

Museums

In Detroit, the **Detroit Historical Museum** (5401 Woodward Ave., 313-833-1805) traces the history of the city from 1701, including the longtime Native American involvement in local history.

In Harbor Springs, the **Chief Andrew J. Blackbird Museum** (368 East Main St., 616-526-7731) is the former home of a prominent Native American, now containing a collection of artifacts and apparel.

Bloomfield Hills has the **Cranbrook Institute of Science** (500 Lone Pine Road, 313-645-3200), which includes a natural history section offering insights into Michigan's Native American history.

Cross Village has the **Great Lakes Indian Museum** (post office, 616-526-6610), while Traverse City has the **Indian Drum Lodge Museum** (Camp Greilick, 4754 Scout Camp Road). Established in the former home of Chief Peter Ringnose, the latter contains a collection of "ceremonial artifacts," wood crafts, and apparel.

In Alpena, the **Jesse Besser Museum** (491 Johnson St., 517-356-2202) is located on the campus of Alpena Community College, and offers exhibits of Native American and northern Michigan history and art.

In Farwell, the **First American Museum** (city offices, 517-588-9927) has a large collection of Native American artifacts, while Frankenmuth has its **Historical Museum** (613 South Main St., 517-652-9701). The latter provides exhibits that show the history of the community, beginning with its role as a Native American mission village. A similar exhibit is offered in Sebewaing at

Luckhard's Museum: The Indian Mission (821 East Main St.), located in the community's 1845 mission building. Here, Native American and pioneer artifacts of the mid-19th century are displayed.

Removal and Return

President Andrew Jackson signed the Indian Removal Act of 1830, which gave the U.S. government permission to "trade" lands east of the Mississippi, the homelands of numerous Native American nations, for unknown territory west of the river. Jackson cloaked his act in words of reassurance to the American Indians, telling them that the move was for their protection. In one sense Jackson was correct, for the oncoming non-Indians were not unlike an avalanche. Vaguely defined areas were quickly becoming official territories, a designation putting them on the threshold of statehood, which was the final goal of aggressive frontier expansion.

As might be imagined, a number of tribal communities did not want to leave their traditional locations, sites of their heritage for countless generations. Some within the American government also felt the Removal Act was unjust and potentially tragic, and this proved to be the case. Michigan's Indian populations faced fewer confrontations than their neighbors to the south and east, however. When Jackson and his Indian Bureau were initially enforcing the policy, the areas of Michigan, Wisconsin, and Minnesota were more or less ignored. The Potawatomi around St. Joseph and Niles were an exception. They were removed.

The Potawatomi were sent away, but they came back–singly, in pairs, in families–to the place where their heritage and the graves of their ancestors lay. By the 1840s, more than 100 Catholic Potawatomi had returned to an area south of Battle Creek. In 1848, the settlers in the area bought land for them, establishing the only "state" reservation in the Upper Midwest. The Potawatomi continue to live in the Athens area, on the holdings of their ancestors.

Treaties eroded the territories long considered Ojibwa or Ottawa land. Beginning in 1798, land was ceded from tribal possession in the upper peninsula, where additional land cessions occurred in 1820, 1836, and 1842. In the lower peninsula, the loss of tribal territory began in 1807, with significant recurrences in 1819, 1821, and 1836. The 1819 treaty with the Ojibwa provided reservation holdings in the Saginaw Valley, but the tribe was continually pressured to give up this land. This finally happened in 1837, after a tragic epidemic nearly wiped out the Saginaw Valley population. The 1855 treaty took yet more land, but resulted in the permanent reservations of today.

Many Potawatomi and Ojibwa felt "homeless" throughout the 19th century. "Strolling" bands were formed of as many as 1,000 people. As the 20th century began, the Potawatomi were finally settled near Hannahville on the Branch

River, near Escanaba, where a reservation exists today.

Here's an interesting facet of Native American history in Michigan: In 1850, Indians were given the right to vote and even to run for office in those counties where the population was predominantly Indian. It would be many years before other Great Lakes states, or even the United States, allowed the nation's original citizens voting rights or the right to serve the broader community.

An Eagle Dance Bustle, as worn at an Oneida powwow.

During the Civil War, Michigan also had the largest federal Indian Agency in the nation, and a number of educational and social innovations were funded in the area by the U.S. government and church denominations. The initiative was short-lived, though. In 1865, there were 32 Indian schools in Michigan. Twenty years later, when the government and church support was drastically cut back, only six schools were left.

The reservations of today are but miniature representations of the vast territories once considered homeland by the Council of Three–the Ottawa, the Ojibwa, and the Potawatomi. For today's traveler exploring Native American heritage and culture, the Michigan reservations are hospitable places.

Reservations

The **Huron Potawatomi Reservation** is the only state-supervised reservation in the Great Lakes area, and it's located in the Calhoun County town of Athens. More specifically, it's found about 40 miles SSW of Jackson and seven miles from Union City, near the intersection of State Highways 60 and 66.

Another Potawatomi reservation, known as the **Hannahville Michigan Potawatomi Reservation**, is located on the upper peninsula. The tribal office is the Hannahville Indian Community (Route 1, 906-466-2342), located about 20

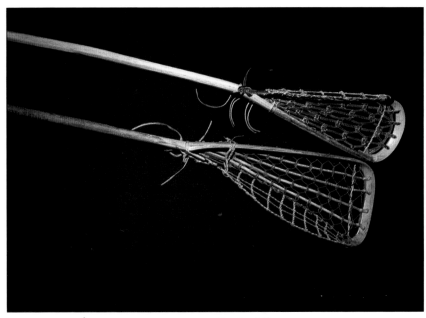

Lacrosse sticks similar to those cleverly used by the Ojibwa in capturing Michilimackinac.

miles west of Escanaba on U.S. Highways 2 and 41. Each year during the last weekend in June, the Hannahville Potawatomi host the **Annual Great Lakes Area Powwow**. Further information is available from the tribal office. The reservation also has a casino where bingo and other games are offered.

The **Grand Traverse Ojibwa Reservation** (616-271-3538) near Suttons Bay is a 300-acre tract with a population of 450 on or near the reservation. The group's tribal council sponsors the **Peshawbestown Powwow** in August, a festivity that includes drumming, dancing, and arts and crafts. The tribe also runs the **Leelanau Sands Casino** and the **Super Bingo Palace**. For information, call 1-800-962-4646.

One other reservation is located on the lower peninsula. The **Isabella Reservation** in Isabella County has its tribal offices at Mt. Pleasant. For information, contact Saginaw Chippewa Tribal Operations (7070 East Broadway, 517-772-5700). U.S. Highway 27 crosses the reservation. During the first weekend in August, the tribe holds its annual **Little Elk's Retreat Traditional Powwow** at the Saginaw Chippewa Campgrounds on Tomah Road. Camping is available through the tribal office. A casino on the reservation offers bingo and other games.

On Whitefish Bay near Sault Ste. Marie is the **Bay Mills Reservation**, located in Chippewa County. The tribal headquarters is in Brimley (Route 1, 906-248-3241). The reservation is located on State Highway 221 north, off Highway 28. A casino on the reservation offers bingo and other games.

Not far away, the **Sault Ste. Marie Reservation** is a 242-acre tract with a population of about 2,500. The tribal council is located in Sault Ste. Marie (206 Greenough St., 906-635-6050), and serves a number of Ojibwa-Chippewa in northern Michigan, among them the people of St. Ignace, Manistique, and Munising. The council sponsors two powwows each summer. The first, called the **Sault Ste. Marie Powwow**, is centered around the Fourth of July weekend and is held on the council grounds on Shunk Road. Another powwow is held in early August. The tribe owns and operates a 46-room hotel off of Interstate 75 called the **Kewadin Inn**, a bingo parlor, and two casinos. For information about the **Vegas Kewadin North** or the **Kewadin Shores** casinos, call 906-632-0530. The tribe operates about 15 other business enterprises in the Sault Ste. Marie vicinity, and an interpretive museum sponsored by the council was scheduled to open in 1992.

Near the community of Watersmeet is the **Lac Vieux Desert Reservation** (Choate Road, 906-358-4585), another small Ojibwa reservation with a population of approximately 350. The group sponsors the annual **Lac Vieux Desert Powwow**, which features traditional dancing, arts and crafts, and foods. The tribe also operates a casino, a bingo parlor, and the **Lac Vieux Desert Gift Shop**, where visitors can watch local artisans at work.

Finally, there is the **Keweenaw Bay Reservation** in Baraga County, also known as the **L'anse Reservation**. The tribal headquarters, called the

Keweenaw Bay Indian Community (Route 1, Box 45, 906-353-6623), is located in Baraga. The **Annual Traditional Powwow** is held at the end of July at the Ojibwa Campground, "Home of the Original Midnight Two-Step World Championship." The Keweenaw Bay Indian Community also has a casino offering bingo and other games.

Councils

Michigan has one of the largest Native American populations in the U.S., an estimated 45,000, and only a small percentage live on the state's reservations. Therefore, there are a number of Native American tribal councils in urban settings, councils providing a variety of outreach services and cultural activities.

The **Grand Rapids Inter-Tribal Council** (756 Bridge NW, 616-774-8331), has for more than three decades hosted the **Annual Grand Valley American Indian Lodge Powwow North** at the Comstock Riverside Park (Monroe Avenue) in early September. For further information, call 616-791-4014 or 616-361-5380. In June, the **Homecoming of the Three Fires Powwow** is held at the same location. Call the council office for further information.

The **Genessee Indian Center** (124 West First St., 313-239-6621) in Flint provides social and economic development services to more than 6,000 Native Americans in six Michigan counties. Outreach programs include housing, education, and health, as well as cultural activities, craft classes, and art exhibits. The center includes an Indian crafts store, and the **Anishinabe Aki Village**, a "museum for the living arts." The center sponsors an annual powwow in Mt. Morris at the Genessee County Fairgrounds, generally held over the Fourth of July weekend. For further information, call the office in Flint.

Powwows

In Algonac, the American Indian Communities Leadership Council (AICLC) holds its **AICLC One Day Indian Festival** in late April at the Algonac Elementary School. For information, call 313-984-3101.

At Big Rapids, **Ferris State University** (Box 27, Rankin Center) holds a powwow in mid-May on the campus at Tom Taggert Field.

A new powwow was initiated recently in Marion. An **Annual Indian Powwow** in late May is held on Kogler's Property. For information, call 616-281-3640 or 616-791-4014.

The Anishinabe Inter-Tribal Council in East Jordan has been holding the **Annual Day of the Eagle Powwow** for more than a decade at the Mill Street Powwow Grounds. For information on the early-June celebration, call 616-536-7583.

In Detroit during the first part of June, the **Annual First People's International Trade Expo and Powwow** happens at the State Fairgrounds. The event is sponsored by the South Eastern Michigan Indians. For powwow information, call 313-756-1350.

The Lansing North American Indian Center (820 West Saginaw, 517-487-5409) sponsors the **Lansing Powwow** in mid-June at Sleepy Hollow State Park.

The **Bay City Powwow** in late July is held at the Bay City Fairgrounds. For more information, call 517-772-5700.

In Burlington in early August, the **Annual Traditional Leonard J. Pamp Powwow** has been held for more than 15 years at 10 1/2 Mile Road. For information, call 616-729-9434.

Early October in Kalamazoo is the occasion of the **Annual Western Michigan University Powwow**. Contact the Reed Field House, 616-349-5387.

Eastern Michigan University has begun sponsoring an annual powwow in early November at the Bowen Field House, put on by the Native American Student Organization and the Multicultural Center. For more information, call 313-487-2379.

Service Organizations

The **Saginaw Inter-Tribal Association** (3239 Christy Way, 517-792-4610) serves the social and health needs of Native Americans in the Saginaw Bay area and provides genealogical referrals. The association also publishes a newsletter, *Bear Talk*.

The **Michigan Agency of the Bureau of Indian Affairs** is located in Sault Ste. Marie (Federal Square Office Plaza, 906-632-6809). Elsewhere, the **Urban Indian Affairs** office (1200 6th Avenue, 8th Floor, 313-256-1633) is located in Detroit. The **Michigan Commission on Indian Affairs** in Lansing is part of the state Department of Management and Budget (300 East Michigan Ave., 517-373-0654).

In the private sector, the **North American Indian Association** (360 John R Drive, 313-963-1710) in Detroit was founded in 1940 and dedicated as a meeting center to preserve and promote Native American culture. The association also assists Native Americans in receiving higher education opportunities, and provides aid in times of need. Also headquartered in Detroit is the **Associated Indians of Detroit** (3901 Cass).

Ironwood is the home of the **All Tribes Indian Center** (820 West Pine St.); in Oak Park there is the **North American Indian Club** (8760 Troy Road); and in Ann Arbor there is **American Indians Unlimited** (515 East Jefferson).

Research and Study Programs

The **Society for Ethnomusicology** in Ann Arbor (313-668-6885) has 2,000 members around the country who are ethnomusicologists, anthropologists, musicologists or lay people interested in the study of Western and non-Western music, including Native American musicology. The society awards an annual Seeger Prize, publishes a triannual journal, and holds an annual conference.

The **Aboriginal Research Club** in West Bloomfield (7090 Valley Brook Road, 313-626-2235) is made up of professional and amateur anthropologists, historians, and ethnologists who are interested in the archaeology of Michigan, including the Great Lakes and Native Americans of the region. The club has its own library.

The **Organization of North American Indian Students** is located in Marquette (University Center, 906-227-2138) on the campus of Northern Michigan University. The organization encourages the pride and identity of American Indian culture and tradition, and seeks to establish communication with Native American communities. It promotes scholarships and the annual Indian Awareness Week.

College courses of study regarding Native American history and heritage are offered at the **University of Michigan** (313-764-7275) in Ann Arbor, through the department of anthropology. There are also Native American exhibits are featured in the university's Museum of Anthropology.

Bay Mills Community College in Brimley, location of the Bay Mills Reservation, provides a curriculum dedicated in part to the culture and language of the Native American people, especially the primary settlers of the area.

Other colleges and universities in Michigan offer periodic courses related to history, ethnology, anthropology, archaeology, and linguistics of Native American peoples.

Fort Mackinac, recaptured by the British and their Native American allies in the War of 1812.

△ **Mound Sites**

● **Attractions**

● **Cities & Towns**

Native Michigan

RED BIRD

6
Wisconsin: Grasses and Waters

The state's name is thought to be a French corruption of the Ojibwa word *wees-kon-san*, which might mean either a "gathering of waters" or a "grassy place." Wisconsin, of course, has both natural ingredients, and both certainly played important roles in the development of Native American cultures within the present-day borders.

The area has been conducive to human habitation since the Wisconsin Glacier began its retreat about 10,000 years ago. Aboriginal immigrants began to enter the territory as it was "evacuated" by the two-mile-thick ice-pack.

It's likely that the Hopewell people or emigrants from the community of Cahokia built what we now call Aztalan. The name was originated by a 19th-century traveler who thought the mound he had rediscovered resembled an Aztec creation. There are many similarities between this and the southern Illinois site. Today, the south central Wisconsin state park is a reconstruction of what archaeologists and cultural anthropologists think might once have been there. What makes the site unique is the fact that it's built not unlike a frontier fort, with poles and logs set into the earth to protect residents from whatever lurked outside. Whereas researchers can only guess whether other sites contained pole walls, Aztalan burned to the ground in its final days, and the clay-like earth was literally baked, retaining the shapes of the log poles it once held.

Aztalan was a small settlement, almost a frontier outpost. Experts believe that no more than 500 people lived there over a two-century period. While it's not a classic, remote and preserved site like Macchu Pichu of Peru or the Mayan temples of Central America, the reconstruction enables the traveler to time-travel, at least for a moment, to what may closely resemble a village of 1200 A.D. Aztalan is located on County Trunk B, off Interstate 94, three miles east of Lake Mills. The park is open year-round, but vehicles may enter only from April 15 until October 15.

In Wisconsin, there is adequate evidence of the 2,000-year-old Mound Builders culture, which was active into the 17th century. The greatest abundance of extant mounds is to be found along the high banks of the Mississippi separating Iowa and Wisconsin. According to estimates, as many as 10,000 mounds once existed in this zone, and Wisconsin has its share of these mysterious and sacred forms. While archaeologists and anthropologists have been justly accused of methodically destroying these sites, the vast majority have literally been plowed under or leveled by farmers, miners, and

The Winnebago warrior Red Bird, whose likeness stands today in High Cliff State Park.

developers, who saw the mounds as obstacles rather than monuments from a lost epoch.

Mounds

Because 5,000 mounds have been identified within its borders, Wisconsin is noted for its many "official" mound sites and parks. At least one source indicates that 98 percent of the known mounds in North America are within the Badger state.

The **Sheboygan Indian Mound Park** (South 12th St. and Panter Ave., 414-459-3444) in Sheboygan contains 18 of an original group of 34 effigy mounds. Called the **Kletzien Mound Group**, these forms originated in the Hopewell era (500 to 1000 A.D.). The mounds are listed in the National Register of Historic Places. The park includes a self-guided mound trail, as well as a nature trail.

Devils Lake State Park (S5975 Park Rd., 608-356-8301) near Baraboo is noted for its 500-foot rock cliffs and its deep lake, but the park also contains a number of effigy mounds, among them the bear and lynx at the northern end of the lake and a bird effigy on the opposite shore. The park's visitor center contains a diorama illustrating the way the Indians constructed the bear mound. Nearby, in downtown Baraboo, is **Man Mound**, one of the few effigy mounds that represents a human figure.

Preserved and protected mounds are located at **High Cliff State Park** (N7475 High Cliff Road, 414-989-1106) on the shore of Lake Winnebago near Menasha, and at nearby **Calumet County Park** (N6150 Cty Trunk EE, 414-439-1008). Both parks are open year-round. Within Menasha itself, the **Menasha Mounds** are located in Smith Park. The three mounds here are thought to represent giant cats or panthers.

Lizard Mound Park near West Bend contains over 30 mounds, most of which are more than a meter tall. The distinctive lizard is augmented by several that apparently represent abstract shapes.

Perrot State Park (608-534-6409), near Trempealeau, is located on the Mississippi River. It's the site of hundreds, perhaps thousands, of mounds. The conical mounds in the park are considered Hopewell earthworks.

Also on the Mississippi, at the conjunction of the Wisconsin River, is **Wyalusing State Park** (608-996-2261), south of Prairie du Chien. On the high ridge above the rivers, visitors will find an outstanding "procession" of mounds–a series of mounds in a row.

In Madison, the "City of Four Lakes," hundreds of mounds are situated on banks and ridges. They're found in disparate and unlikely locations. On the grounds of **Mendota State Hospital**, for example, a six-foot-high bird the length of two football fields still rests. Others are located on the rolling hills of the Blackhawk Country Club, scattered on the University of Wisconsin

Stand Rock, a historic site near Wisconsin Dells.

campus, or found in various suburban settings.

At **Fort Atkinson**, 45 miles from Madison, sits a very unique earthwork, the **Panther Intaglio**. This impressive, sizeable cat was carved in the surface of the land, and even today the intaglio is about one foot deep. It may be guarding the traditional raised mounds that are found nearby, or it may have been the expression of a singular mound builder. For information, contact the Fort Atkinson Chamber of Commerce, 89 N. Main. The phone is 414-563-3210.

In 1990, the **State Historical Society of Wisconsin** (816 State St., 608-262-1368), headquartered in Madison, completed a re-evaluation of various documents and maps held in its extensive Native American collection. The Historical Society and the **Wisconsin Department of Natural Resources' Bureau of Parks and Recreation** (608-266-2181) in Madison can provide travelers with further information about existing evidence of the mound building cultures that thrived in Wisconsin for so many centuries.

The **Office of Wisconsin Tourism Development** (123 West Washington Ave., 608-266-2161) in Madison has published several magazines that not only provide suggested tours, but indicate sources for other information. The publications also offer information about attractions, lodging, and additional features that may be near historic Native American sites.

Basswood twine, used in making rope, clothing, and baskets.

Prehistoric Parks

The **Ice Age Interpretive Center** (Interstate Park, Highway 35) in St. Croix Falls is part of Wisconsin's first state park, created in 1900. The center presents photographs, murals, a film, and other information about the Ice Age that literally covered most of Wisconsin. The park also includes archaeological sites.

Copper Culture State Park (U.S. 41 and State Highway 22) near Oconto is one of few official parks honoring the 5000-year-old culture that used copper so extensively. The state park came about after burial sites including copper weapons and implements were discovered. The copper items were tested, and were found to be much older than Adena and Hopewell objects found at other locations. Further analysis revealed that these Native Americans were using pure natural copper at about the same time that people in other parts of the world were using it. However, Wisconsin's people did not use other minerals to harden or change the copper to brass or other metals. The state park is open year-round.

Gullickson's Glen near Black River Falls consists of a deep sandstone ravine where early residents etched petroglyphs of the various animals and birds, as well as human figures. The figures include an eagle dancer, a hunter with a bow, a thunderbird, buffalo, cranes, turkeys, and elk. The Wisconsin Historical Society in Madison is the overseer of the historical site.

The Nations

Half a dozen identified Native American nations exist in Wisconsin. Before considering these, however, it's important to note that, according to the 1990 U.S. census, more than half of the state's Native Americans live in non-reservation communities such as Milwaukee, Madison, Green Bay, and La Crosse. Therefore, following the portraits of reservations or tribal entities, we'll provide a listing of some of the more prominent events that take place in Wisconsin's major cities. In general, Native Wisconsin Indians maintain family and cultural ties as well as tribal membership, whether they're living in Milwaukee, Cleveland, Dallas, Los Angeles, or New York City. They return for family occasions and for annual powwows. They vote in tribal elections with absentee ballots. Quite often, they retire to the reservation once their "mainstream" work is completed.

The Wisconsin tribal societies, or nations, include the Menominee, the Winnebago, the Chippewa (Ojibwa), the Oneida, the Stockbridge-Munsee, and the Potawatomi. There are six bands of Ojibwa, located in Lac du Flambeau, Mole Lake, St. Croix, Bad River, Lac Court Oreilles, and Red Cliff. According to traditional legend, the Ojibwa, the Potawatomi, and Canada's Ottawa tribes are related–known as the "Three Fires."

Menominee

Historians consider the Menominee the longest continuous residents of the state. The Menominee have always been a Wisconsin tribal nation, and archaeological evidence of their presence extends to 5,000 years ago. At one time, the Menominee people called most of the eastern half of Wisconsin and Michigan's Upper Peninsula their homeland. Over the centuries, as incoming tribes pushed each other across preferred hunting, fishing, and gathering territories, the Menominee saw their homeland diminish.

For the Menominee, there was a central gathering place or village, *Mini'Kani*, established at the mouth of the Menominee River, which literally divides the Upper Peninsula of Michigan and Wisconsin, and today is the location of Menominee, Michigan and Marinette, Wisconsin.

The Menominee people stayed basically within the region proscribed by the river, but like its flowage they ventured southward as far as the current site of Milwaukee. When the first Europeans visited the Menominee homeland in about 1630, an estimated 5,000 Menominees were living within an area about the size of contemporary Wisconsin.

The Menominee were a peaceful people. They thrived on the bounties of the seasons, endured the long, white winters, and built upon the natural elements that were constantly replenished with each season. They were not an isolated people, for their harvests and crafts were known to other Native American nations. They were therefore part of the intricate trading network that existed long before the arrival of the Europeans.

There is no question that the coming of the French and English to the northern areas of the continent created social and economic problems. Native American tribes of the eastern region, which had already begun western migrations, collided with established and generally peaceful populations wherever they went. Wisconsin and Minnesota were territorial battlegrounds for more than a century, as eastern Dakota and Ojibwa tribes sought to establish their presence in lands that they considered open to exploitation.

While the "interlopers" were Woodland Indians, they were also accustomed to war as a means of defining territorial boundaries. These new arrivals were quite willing to fight for areas that the passive Sauk, Mesquakie, Winnebago, and Menominee had long enjoyed via cooperation and coexistence.

Enter Europe's most terrible weapon, a weapon more terrible than gunpowder: epidemics. Smallpox and other diseases decimated tribal communities in the early 18th century. There were few tribes not infected, and whose populations were not cut down. Epidemics would haunt Native Americans for the next two centuries.

Meanwhile, confronted by territorial challenges, the Menominee built a new tribal center at the base of Green Bay. This would later cause a conflict with the Winnebago and the Potawatomi over the slender peninsula that is now Door County.

The greatest number of "outsiders" were Ojibwas who came out of the land north of the Great Lakes and settled, first in the Bad River and Madeline Island area on the southern shore of what is now Lake Superior.

Many Menominee, moving to settlements west of the great bay that was the site of their traditional origins, joined Ojibwa who were migrating south in their quest for food and resources. This interspersing of cultures was not without precedent–nor did it destroy either tribe's background and heritage. Later, as Winnebagos sought to retain their Wisconsin ties, intermarriage would expand the boundaries of Woodland Indian culture.

Like other Woodland Indians, the Menominee were distinguished by their domestic structures, by their water craft, by their winter travel, and by their utilization of natural crops. They lived in two kinds of dwellings. Summer homes were rectangular, covered by elm and cedar bark and supported by pole frames lashed together. They were open, allowing air to flow through freely. However, the Menominee winter home was quite different. Called *wiikiop*, it was a place built with warmth in mind. A fire was built in its center, and a small hole allowed smoke to escape. A circle of stones surrounded the fire, retaining heat and protecting the residents from straying sparks.

Menominees made two kinds of canoes as well–birchbark and dugout. The birchbark craft were lightweight, built for four people, and were easily portaged from flowage to flowage or lake to lake. The dugouts were built to travel on the more substantial and variable waters of Green Bay and the larger

A porcupine quill basket created by the Ottawa.

lakes in the region. They carried more weight, more people, and more cargo. Birchbark canoes were built with cedar and birch, while the dugouts were generally sculpted out of butternut tree trunks.

The Menominee did not hide from winter. They designed intricate devices to wear on their feet and to carry them over deep snows: We call these devices snowshoes. Ash frames were interwoven with leather webbing, and thongs were added to restrain the feet. Like the canoe, the snowshoe was adopted as a primary means of travel by Europeans who entered Woodland Indian territories. Both are still being crafted, and the greatest value is placed upon those that are hand-crafted in the traditional way.

It could be asserted that the Menominee were not warlike because they were not threatened by shortages of resources. The Great Spirit filled the rivers, the lakes, the marshes, and the forests with fish, game, vegetables, and fruits. The duty of the Menominee was to hunt, fish, and gather in order to sustain the people. Corn, beans, squash, and pumpkins were grown in family or tribal gardens. Berries were gathered for sweetening and seasoning, just as maple trees were tapped for the syrup that created the sweetest of sugars. Nuts thrived in the woodland countryside–chestnuts, hickory nuts, hazelnuts–as did potatoes, onions, cranberries, mushrooms, and grapes. The

Menominee drummers participate in a Children's Education Day.

stalks of Jack-in-the-pulpit were a special treat, and wild herb tea was a traditional beverage.

However popular these foods were, the Menominee specialized in the harvesting of wild rice. In fact, they harvested so much that other tribes called them *Mano'min ini'niwuk*, the Wild Rice People. The gathering of the rice was an autumnal activity. Women paddled canoes into the rice fields of certain lakes, and by maneuvering the craft in a special way, shook the rice kernels into the canoes and onto mats. The rice was dried in the sun and threshed through a skin over a hole in the ground. Later, winnowing would be done with a carved birchbark tray which, when tossed in the air, separated husks from grains. The rice's special role was as a resource providing sustenance throughout even the longest, darkest winters. This traditional food-gathering is still practiced.

Treaties and agreements with the American government fundamentally shaped the fate of the Menominee people. The first treaty was signed in 1817, and by 1848 the people had ceded or sold 9.5 million acres of territory. At one point, the U.S. government intended to force the Menominee to relocate in Minnesota. After six years of debate between the two nations, a decision allowed them to stay in Wisconsin, within the confines of 275,000 acres covering a dozen township squares.

This allotted space became the Menominee Reservation, located in the northeastern sector of the state. Still, their land was considered of great value, and the tribe was constantly plagued by outside forces and pressures. In the mid-19th century, Wisconsin was a primary source of lumber for many of the new towns and cities in the Midwestern frontier, and the land of the Menominee harbored some of the nation's finest forests.

The tribe did not yield to outsiders. Instead, they developed their own lumber resources, and for the next 50 years built upon several generations of experience. By 1908, the Menominee were able to pay for their own community services, including schools and health care facilities, and had built a sawmill on the reservation. The year 1908 was an important one, for Wisconsin began then to regulate timber harvesting and to manage the tribe's lumber business.

The next half-century was not kind to the Menominees. Millions of dollars in tribal revenues were lost due to state mismanagement, and decades of litigation were required to recover a percentage of the loss. Also, the Bureau of Indian Affairs and the Department of the Interior were experimenting with different programs intended to "mainstream" Native Americans. A policy of "termination" was instituted, meaning that the reservations of certain tribes would be terminated in order to make the people responsible for their own lives. The policy mandated payment of income taxes to county, state, and federal governments.

Ironically, when the Menominee finally won their lawsuit against Wisconsin and received a settlement of $7.65 million, the BIA put the tribe on its termination list. The Menominee fought termination on the grounds that many of the people were not in positions of self-sufficiency. Time was needed, they argued, to develop educational institutions, business experience, and local government structures.

Washington listened to the protests, and promised that each member of the tribe would get a cash bonus when the reservation was terminated. In 1960, President Eisenhower signed the Menominee Termination Act. Via that stroke of the presidential pen, Wisconsin gained another county and the Menominee lost the reservation and support system upon which they had become dependent.

The experiment did not work. The developmental base in Menominee County was not sufficient. The tribal corporation, Menominee Enterprises, once a thriving corporation, was being bankrupted by taxes paid to the county and the state. The corporation was forced to sell land to pay off debts.

Again, protests were registered. These were mostly diplomatic, but there were occasional, violent reactions to the futility of the situation. Finally, in 1973, President Nixon signed an act restoring reservation status to the Menominee. Menominee County is still shown on the state map, but it is also the Menominee Reservation. There are now 234,000 acres of Menominee land. The forest still provides sustenance, as do the many lakes and rivers.

Today, more than 4,000 Menominee live on the reservation. More than half of this population is of high school age. A full primary and secondary school system exists within reservation boundaries. The major economic development entities are the tribal government's planning committee and Menominee Tribal Enterprises, Inc.

The Menominee Tribal Legislature is a nine-member body, including the tribal chairman. It governs tribal activities and oversees developmental projects on the reservation, working in conjunction with Menominee Tribal Enterprises. One of the reservation's chief attractions is the **Menominee Logging Museum**, which documents Menominee involvement with that industry and is operated by the tribe. Another tribal business that attracts tourists involves the rental of rafts, canoes, kayaks, and tubes, with which visitors can travel through the reservation on the beautiful Wolf River. For information about the reservation, call 715-799-5114.

Menominee Tribal Bingo and the **Menominee Nation Casino** (800-421-3077/715-799-4495/715-799-4593) are located on the reservation in Keshena. The casino and bingo hall are open seven days a week, and a full-service kitchen provides snacks or complete meals. Information about a "Stay and Play Motel Package" is available by calling 800-752-0063.

Winnebago

Today's Winnebago have no reservation in Wisconsin, but Winnebago communities are found in ten Wisconsin counties and in Minnesota, and what is considered "tribal land" is located in half a dozen Wisconsin communities. Over the years, a tradition of intermarriage between Winnebago and other tribes has also set them apart–from each other and from nations with reservation identities.

At one point in their history, the Siouan people chose to divide their destinies. One group emigrated west to prairies beyond the great rivers that divided the continent; the other group stayed in the land of forests and streams, rivers and lakes.

The Winnebago's prehistoric, traditional name was *Hochungra*. The name is variously interpreted to mean "Big Voiced People," "People of the Parent Speech," and "Big Fish People." The Winnebago language does not specify which is correct. A slang term used by the tribe, however, is "Hochunk," which can mean either "big voice" or "big fish."

The "Winnebago" designation comes from early French explorers who undoubtedly misinterpreted the Hochungra language and came up with a name that meant "People of the Sea."

A traditional Winnebago cradle.

From the Winnebago, an otter medicine bag.

The group's first contact with Europeans came in 1634, when Jean Nicolet, French agent for North America's Gov. Champlain, visited the people living in the Red Banks area of Green Bay. At the time, the Winnebago/Hochungra had divided territory with various tribes, including the Menominee and the Potawatomi. Later, armed struggles would occur between these nations, but in Nicolet's time all was relatively peaceful.

Smallpox was a European import that changed Native American cultures in far more calamitous ways than the blankets, beads, and trinkets that were exchanged for furs and exploratory information. The Winnebago were among the first to suffer from major population losses and the great infusion of fear that is the bedfellow of disease.

An incident that took place in the mid-18th century had direct impact on the strength and tribal pride of the Winnebago. It also provided the name of Wisconsin's most popular contemporary tourist attraction–Door County. Winnebagos occupying the calm harbor at the base of what is now Green Bay maintained, as a result, a certain territorial superiority over much of the upper peninsula. However, a very insular, protected island stood at the tip of the fingerlike peninsula jutting into Lake Michigan, inhabited by a tribe of the Potawatomi. Because of the rough waters of the lake on the passageway to Green Bay, the island became a favorite stopping place for various explorers and traders.

At about the time the Pilgrims were landing at Plymouth Rock, some 1,000

Potawatomi were living on the 20-square-mile island atop the narrow spit of land that separated the great lake from the quiet bay. According to legend, the possessive Winnebagos wanted exclusive trading rights with the French, and the Potawatomi were not willing to cooperate.

The story has it that Winnebago warriors launched their canoes one day, probably from a spot near the present ferry landing at Newport. However, the currents and winds were so horrendous that the entire Winnebago group was lost. When French traders heard the tale, and recalled their own losses in the small strait, it was named *"Le Porte des Mortes Passage."* Subsequently, "Death's Door" became the traveler's delight, Door County.

At this time, the power of the Winnebago began to wane. Incoming Ojibwa tribes enforced a southern exodus that took the Winnebago far from the land of their origin. However, they maintained their traditional practices, which included structural design, clothing and craft work, and the woodlands lifestyle. Nor was their spiritual heritage changed.

The process of displacement, in fact, was familiar to many of the Native American groups that called Wisconsin home at one time or another. The Kickapoo, Illinois, Iowa, Cree, Sauk, Ottawa, Fox, Huron, Miami, and Mascouten nations were residents, and each in turn was displaced by a larger, stronger, more aggressive group.

As the new, European-settled nation evolved, the group that became the largest, strongest, and most aggressive was the government of the United States. Native American nations were forced to negotiate treaties controlling their movements or ceding their rights of occupation.

The Winnebagos found themselves in the unfortunate position of having their rug pulled from beneath them. Their initial treaty in 1829 was the result of a plea-bargain. A Winnebago warrior, Red Bird, had retaliated against what he felt were territorial violations by incoming lead miners. He and a few followers took their revenge upon a group of settlers. The threat of a U.S. reprisal caused the Winnebago leadership to negotiate a treaty sparing Red Bird's life in exchange for land that the miners wanted.

Eight years later, the Winnebago had ceded or given away most of their territory. In 1837, a great lapse in communication occurred concerning another treaty. The leadership unknowingly signed a paper specifying that the entire tribe would move out of Wisconsin Territory and across the Mississippi River, into space allotted in the Iowa Territory.

When the real terms of the treaty were understood by the Winnebago, a multiple split ensued within tribal families. Some Winnebago went to what is now Minnesota; others went to South Dakota; and others traveled to what is now Nebraska, where a large settlement remains today. However, many returned to Wisconsin, to the discomfort of regulators in Washington.

In 1874, the federal government made its last attempt to relocate the Wisconsin Winnebagos. The resultant deaths among the old and infirm, who were being transported in rickety boxcars, focused considerable public attention on the matter. Legislators then created a unique agreement with the Wisconsin Winnebago: Each family was allotted a quarter section (40 acres) in western Wisconsin, to be used for farming.

However, many of the Winnebago plots were situated on marshland, and were subsequently lost due to unpaid taxes. Because the Winnebago had not been accorded reservation status, they were not allowed to govern themselves, or to build their own legal framework. Sixty years later, a number of elders sought formal organization by writing a tribal constitution, hoping to be recognized as their kin in Nebraska had been. Fifteen years passed before the Winnebago of Wisconsin were granted anything approaching tribal status, and it was not until 1961 that a Winnebago Business Committee was formed. With this institution in place, they could at last gain access to health, education, and fundamental welfare.

Seven Wisconsin communities contain significant Winnebago populations: Wittenburg, Fairchild, Black River Falls, Nekoosa, Tomah, Wisconsin Dells, and La Crosse. The tribally enrolled population is estimated at 2,200, and about 50 percent of those are school-age. Though no prescribed sovereign land exists for the state's Winnebago, 4500 acres are allotted as 40-acre homesteads and 554 acres have been set aside for tribal entities.

For many years, the relative isolation of Winnebago families and communities led to various plans for achieving self-sufficiency. At Wisconsin Dells, Winnebago have created a cottage industry of exceptional beadwork creations and baskets that are sold to visitors.

Two of the state's top tourist attractions are found in Wisconsin Dells, and both are operated by the Winnebago people. **Stand Rock Ceremonial** (Stand Rock Rd., 608-254-6774) provided long-ago travelers with a moment of derring-do as a buckskin-clad warrior lept from one flat rock to another; later, a great German shepherd would make the difficult leap. Today Stand Rock stands alone as beneath it, amidst the picturesque dells along the Wisconsin River, Winnebago men, women, and children perform traditional Native American dances from mid-June through Labor Day. This is the nightly **Winnebago Ceremonial**, which spotlights tribal dancing, drumming, and singing.

The **Winnebago Indian Museum** (3889 River Rd., 608-254-2268) is a Winnebago chief's private collection, expanded by his children to include memorabilia of Winnebago life as well as items from other tribes. The museum began as a roadside stand enabling the family to sell beadwork and basketry, but the chief was a collector of arrowheads, clothing, photographs, pottery, baskets, and other treasures, so the collection grew. The family still sells traditional Winnebago crafts, but it also offers one of the Midwest's best collections of contemporary jewelry and crafts.

Three Winnebago casinos operate in Wisconsin. In Black River Falls, **Sands Indian Games** (Hwy 54 east off I-94, 800-657-4621) is open seven days

The Winnebago Indian Museum showcases the private collection of a Winnebago chief, as well as contemporary jewelry and crafts.

a week. In Wisconsin Dells, the **Ho-Chunk Bingo Casino** (Hwy 12 south, 800-362-8404 or 800-356-9268) is also open seven days a week. The **Rainbow Bingo Casino** is located in Nekoosa (Creamery Rd. and County Trunk G, 800-236-4560) is the newest of the three facilities, and is open year-round.

Ojibwa

During the pre-Columbian epoch, there was a meaningful westward migration of the Anishinabe people from what is now called the Gulf of the St. Lawrence River. The Anishinabe would later be divided into the Ojibwa, the Potawatomi, and the Ottawa tribes. According to Anishinabe history the Megis Shell, a kind of seashell, appeared five times to the people, rallying them and indicating where they should go. The people moved further westward each time, across the shores of the Great Lakes. Ultimately, the migration divided the people into three different tribes. The Ojibwa settled on a point of land extending into what we call Lake Superior. The land was called *Shagawaumikong*, today named Chequamegon. Later, the Ojibwa found a special island called *Moningwanekaning*, shown on current maps as Madeline Island.

Those who have retraced Anishinabe accounts of the five migratory steps–covering about five centuries–believe that the people who arrived at

Madeline Island did so while Columbus was dropping anchor off the northern coast of Jamaica in the Caribbean. According to the Megis shell account, the Ojibwa went to the island as keepers of the faith of the Anishinabe; the Potawatomi settled on the peninsula of northern Michigan as the keepers of the sacred fire; and the Ottawa settled in the Sault Ste. Marie area as Anishinabe providers or traders.

The discovery of furs by the French at the time of the Pilgrims' arrival in Massachusetts Bay Colony provided the Ojibwa nation with power and currency. The trading between the two nations included commercial items of value to other Native Americans, but also involved weaponry as yet unavailable to the Ojibwa's southern neighbors. In fact, as long as the French controlled northern trading latitudes, the Ojibwa appeared to have a lock on regional supremacy. Their furs brought them European material goods, including firearms. Their new tribal name, Ojibwa, was given to them during this period by other Native Americans who knew they could always be identified by the moccasins they wore. Their tightly stitched pieces of leather had a special puckered look. In the Anishinabe language, the word for "puckered" was *ojibway*.

By the time the first French explorer, Etienne Brule, visited Madeline Island in the early 1600s, the Ojibwa were experiencing overpopulation, and a number of people had moved to the mainland. Before long, several trading posts were established on the shores of Cheqaumegon Bay. Relations between the French and the Ojibwa were amicable, and today many tribal members carry French names that can be traced back to the earliest days of contact.

The Ojibwa's subsequent expansion into the coastal hinterland was guided most often by a clan that had decided to find its own territory for trapping, hunting, fishing, and rice-gathering. As the tribe became decentralized, confrontations with other nations increased. The Ojibwa battled most often with the Sioux and the Fox, who had been enemies even before the Ojibwa arrived at Madeline Island. The French rifles were a reckoning force as the Ojibwa clans moved south and west.

The connection between the clans and the island of origin was not severed, however, as annual migrations became part of the Ojibwa medicine lodge rituals and religion, known as *Midewiwin*. This religious belief was founded in the earliest days of the Anishinabe, and the symbols of the otter and the Megis Shell are central to its practice. Another aspect involves using natural elements for medicinal purposes. *Midewiwin* links the elders of the tribe and their knowledge of Mother Earth with protection of the environment and emerging Ojibwa generations. Under this belief, it is critical to respect one's place and surroundings, and to understand the eternal connection between the

A storage area within the re-created Aztalan stockade.

natural and spiritual worlds.

An Ojibwa story explains how each clan was conceived. During the great flood, six human beings arose from the waters. In reality they were creatures of natural life, but the first one to look at the others died, as if struck by lightning. Through this death, the others learned that respect and downcast vision would save them. They returned the deceased creature to the waters, and became the human community.

The five original beings eventually became five clans of the Ojibwa: the Crane or Echomaker Clan; the Loon Clan; the Bear Clan; the Marten Clan; and the Catfish Clan. Over the years, the clans fostered sub-clans, among them the reindeer, wolf, pike, lynx, eagle, rattlesnake, moose, black duck, sturgeon, beaver, gull, and hawk. These groupings would have special meaning when six reservations were eventually established in Wisconsin.

By the time of the so-called French and Indian War–really a war between the French and the English–the area in which the Ojibwa settled had become valuable territory, for commerce and for settlement. The Ojibwa's connection with the French did not go unnoticed, and battles took place between the Ojibwa and the English for many years. The quest for furs did not stop, though, and the North West Fur Company, the Hudson's Bay Company, and John Jacob Astor's enterprises competed for the Ojibwa harvest along the trade routes.

By the time of the American Revolution, westward migration of European immigrants had begun in earnest. Challenges to Native American sovereignty meant that nations were forced to move from their traditional territories, in turn causing other groups to move further west or north. While the settling of the United States created opportunities for many, it was also a traumatic time for those who regarded their homelands as part of their sacred heritage.

In 1830, President Andrew Jackson decided to settle the "Indian problem." He signed the Indian Removal Act, which stated that all Native Americans living within the boundaries of the United States and its territories should be moved beyond the Mississippi River. That included the Ojibwa.

Needless to say, the Ojibwa living in Michigan, Wisconsin and Minnesota did not want to leave their tribal homelands–places they had known for hundreds of years. An Ojibwa envoy to Washington, D.C., was successful for a time in keeping the Ojibwa off the removal list. In fact, the emissaries and chiefs were successful in their negotiations, and were able to tell the federal government not only where they did not want to go, but where they wanted to stay.

In 1854 a treaty was signed that provided two sites for the Ojibwa in Michigan, five in Wisconsin, and two in Minnesota. The Wisconsin reservations were located at Bad River, Lac Courte Oreilles, Lac du Flambeau, Red Cliff and Mole Lake. Rights to hunt, fish, and gather foods were granted in this treaty by the famous phrase, "as long as the rivers will flow and the grass will grow."

Land ownership was a little-understood notion to many Native Americans, who believed that Mother Earth was not something that could be possessed, enscribed on paper, documented in legal terms, or defined by a map. In fact, Chief Yabanse, the leader of the St. Croix Ojibwa, chose not to attend the 1854 treaty negotiations. He had already been promised that his people could stay where they were as long as nobody made any trouble. The chief trusted the earlier agreements, and did not want to make the long trip. As a result the St. Croix were left out of the picture, were not recognized by the government, and received no land allotment or reservation territory. For 80 years, they would be known as "the Lost Tribe of the Ojibwa," and even when land was granted to the St. Croix in 1934, it would amount to just 1700 acres.

Ojibwa Bands and Reservations

There are six Ojibwa (Chippewa) reservations in Wisconsin, and each has its own identity and history.

Bad River Band

The Ojibwa originally settled on the shores of Lake Superior, known to them as *Gitchi Gamig*. Specifically, they inhabited a spit of land jutting out into the bay that was called *Shagawaumikong*. A more protected site was found on Madeline Island, but three centuries ago, the Loon Clan volunteered to move back to the original settlement. The move was designed to ensure protection of Ojibwa territory.

What today is called the Bad River was then "Mashkizeebee," or "River of the Swamp," and "Gitigoning," or "Old Gardens." At the intersection of the Bad River and the White River, there is an extremely fertile delta, level and ideal for domestic agriculture. The Loon Clan settled here, where nature provided an abundance of maple trees for sugarbushing and ponds that grew succulent wild rice.

A Protestant missionary, Rev. Leonard Wheeler, moved to Madeline Island in 1841. Four years later he led a small congregation to join the others in the vicinity of Ashland, near the intersection of the two rivers. Wheeler called the settlement *Odanah*, meaning simply "village" in Anishinabe. A later misinterpretation of language led to the designation "Bad River."

Bad River Ojibwa farmed their own plots, but they also worked as copper miners in Michigan's Upper Peninsula, handled sawmills, and became sailors on Lake Superior. A century and a half after the missionary attempted to mainstream these people, Odanah remains the central community, and agriculture remains essential to the Ojibwa economy.

The reservation's population stands at about 1,800, with about 40 percent being of school age. The area allotted to the group is 56,697 acres, amounting to about half of the original reservation.

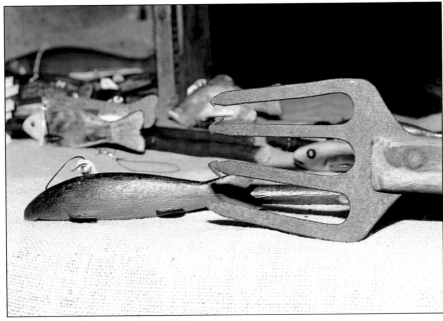

A fish decoy and spear used by the Ojibwa.

The band operates **Bad River Bingo** (Bad River Tribal Center, Hwy 2, 715-682-4134) in Odanah, open Wednesday and Friday evenings. The community also contains convenience stores, a day care center, and a wood products factory. A number of Bad River Ojibwa work as fishermen on Lake Superior.

The **Great Lakes Indian Fish and Wildlife Commission** (715-682-6619) is headquartered in Odanah. The GLIFWC represents the thirteen Ojibwa groups in Wisconsin, Michigan, and Minnesota. The facility serves as an important scientific resource for Great Lakes and inland lakes fisheries. It also focuses on the traditional and historical practices of the Ojibwa, and studies the multitude of treaties that have been signed by the Anishinabe.

Red Cliff Band

Members of the Loon Clan also emigrated to the peninsula directly west of Madeline Island. Two small bays, now called Raspberry and Frog, were easily accessible to the island's central culture. Because the clan's chief was Anton Buffalo, the site was called Buffalo Bay, later officially designated Red Cliff because of the reddish color of the soil.

An 1887 treaty determined that the reservation would be divided into separate units of 80 acres per adult. Typically, poorer tribal members sold their holdings to aggressive speculators, and the size of the reservation was continually diminished. Red Cliff Ojibwa began a sawmill in 1897, replacing one that had burned down twenty years earlier. In 1934, when the logging industry on Red Cliff moved to Canada, and as the federal government passed the Indian Reorganization Act, the band was allowed to organize its own government and constitution. Two years later, the first tribal council was elected.

Tribal members worked for neighboring farmers and fishermen. They learned how to run fishing tugs on Lake Superior, became proficient, and purchased older boats from people who were once their employers. The tribe now owns a fishery, the Buffalo Bay Fish Company, which purchases fish from more than two dozen fishermen, most of whom are Red Cliff Ojibwa.

Tribally-owned enterprises include a campground and marina, and a tribal cultural center showcases Red Cliff history and crafts. In addition, the **First American Prevention Center** develops alcohol and drug abuse treatment curricula for counselors and school districts, and provides consultation services for districts that are developing such programs.

The Red Cliff-operated **Bingo on the Bay** (Hwy 13, 715-779-5825) in Bayfield is open evenings on Thursdays and Saturdays, and opens at noon on Sundays.

The **Red Cliff Tribal Museum** (715-779-5609 or 715-779-5805) is located within the tribal Arts and Crafts Cultural Center in Bayfield. The museum contains historical information and exhibits.

Lac du Flambeau Band

As the clans began to leave Madeline Island, the Crane Clan was led by Sha da wish, son of the great Wabishki Ajijak, or White Crane, who was the original head of the clan. Clan members tried living at several locations, from a place called Turtle Portage near today's Mercer, Wisconsin, to Trout Lake, near today's Boulder Junction, before settling at the headwaters of the Wisconsin River. By that time, the group was led by Sha da wish's son, "Sharpened Stone."

The site that gives the people their name, Lac du Flambeau, was the French description of a practice that made clan members famous throughout northern Wisconsin. Other Native Americans, including Ojibwa, called this clan *Wa Swa Gon*, the Torch People, and their home *Wa Swa Gon ing*, or "place of the Torch People." Tribal history tells of a time when the people first arrived and began to build their village. They soon learned to fish by torchlight at night and, as time passed and visitors came to the area, clan members became recognized as Torch People. When French traders saw the night fishing, they called the place and the people Lac du Flambeau, or Lake of the Torches.

Fishing has been an Ojibwa tradition. The Lac du Flambeau Ojibwa have maintained a fishery on the reservation for more than 50 years, raising fish to release in the lakes and streams of Wisconsin, and for sale to neighboring communities and businesses. The tribe operates a number of businesses, ranging from a successful bingo hall and casino to a new supermarket and an electronics manufacturing firm. Its location in north-central Wisconsin has also provided the tribe with access to some of the best forests in the nation, so the lumber industry has long been a part of Lac du Flambeau life and livelihood.

The Lac du Flambeau recently completed a **Museum and Cultural Center** (Highway D, 715-588-3333). The center is open to the public, and its exhibits depict historical aspects of the Lac du Flambeau. A donation is requested upon entrance, and no photographs are allowed.

The tribe maintains a special outdoor performance area called the **Lac du Flambeau Indian Bowl** (Highway D, 715-588-3346), which is used for pow-wows and related events to which the public is invited. Visitors will also find a replicated **Chippewa Indian Village** in the town of Lac du Flambeau that provides an opportunity to learn about *Wa Swa Gon* history.

Today more than 1,500 Lac du Flambeau Ojibwa live on the 45,000-acre reservation. About 40 percent are of school age. Like the other Ojibwa tribes in Wisconsin, the Lac du Flambeau band is governed by a tribal council, and the tribal organization is the Lac du Flambeau Community Development Corporation. For general information, call 715-588-3303.

Lac du Flambeau Tribal Bingo (Highway 47 North, 800-447-4688 from Wisconsin) is located in the town of Lac du Flambeau. The hall is open Tuesday through Saturday. **Lake of the Torches Casino** (Highway D, 800-447-4688) is nearby, and is open Wednesday through Sunday.

One of the most interesting attractions within the community is the **Lac du Flambeau Fish Hatchery** (Hwy 47 North, 715-588-3303), which is open daily from May until August and charges a minimal fee for sure-catch fishing, no license required. Frustrated fisherfolk who have traveled to the north-woods to catch fish, and whose only luck has been bad, can change their luck on the reservation.

Lac Courte Oreilles Band

Members of the Bear Clan of Madeline Island decided to stake out territory they had named when an Ottawa was found frozen in one of its lakes. *Ottawasawasii'i gii' i goning* literally means "the Place Where They Found the Ottawa." The Bear Clan was noted among Ojibwa for the traditional willingness of its members to confront danger and the unknown. A story illustrates this in describing the Bear Clan's journey to the area in which they settled. While they were winter camping, one of the children died. The group vowed as a result to stay there permanently, choosing to ignore the threats of the Sioux, who considered the place their territory.

As the end of the 18th century approached, the English North West Fur Company staked out certain claims in the Great Lakes region, all of which had

Bingo! Lac du Flambeau–style.

French origins: Fond du Lac, Lac du Flambeau, Folles Avoine, and Lac Courtereille. The English, winners of the French and Indian War, were not opposed to hiring French trappers and traders to work the "outback." Thus, historians encounter names like Cadotte, Cotte, St. Germain, Beauleau, Roussain–names that also became part of the Ojibwa rolls.

One of the most prominent Frenchmen of the era was Dr. Jean Baptiste Corbin, a refugee of the French Revolution who chose to work for the Astor Fur Company rather than facing the guillotine. One of the first things Corbin did in the New World was to establish a trading post at *Ottawasawassisi' i gii' i goning*, where he became known as *Nitaa Bii' idge*, or "the Writer," because he was constantly making notes in his journal. Sadly, when the good doctor/trader moved to his second home on Madeline Island, a fire destroyed his writings. Dr. Corbin married a woman from the Lac Courte Oreilles, and descendants today bear his name.

The tribal name, Lac Courte Oreilles, was provided by French traders, who were always searching for ways to distinguish one group of Native Americans from another so there would be no mistakes made in their contracts and business arrangements, or to avoid those who were unfriendly. Translated simply, the name meant "Lake of the Short Ears." Ojibwa who lived

A dancer teaches kids and adult onlookers the "Fish Dance."

in the area did not practice the tradition of wearing heavy earrings, which could stretch ear lobes to a considerable degree. When an 1854 treaty was signed, the people adopted the name provided by the French.

The reservation's name points to one particular lake, but tribal villages were established in several places, such as New Post, Signor, Whitefish, and Round Lake. Today several community sites exist within the reservation. Some locate the shopping center, others identify homes and schools, or the site of an annual powwow.

The Lac Courte Oreilles operate the only Native American radio station in Wisconsin. **WOJB** is owned by News From Indian Country Communications, which also publishes one of the few Native American newspapers that covers national issues, News from Indian Country. The tribe maintains a complete school system, including a two-year community college. These educational opportunities are available to nearly 2,000 tribal members on the reservation.

The tribal government follows the Ojibwa tradition of a seven-member council and a chairman, a body that in turn oversees the operations of the Lac Courte Oreilles Business Corporation. The corporation operates a bingo hall and casino, as well as a campground, a cultural center, resorts, and various construction enterprises. News from Indian Country publishes the only Native American gaming guide in the U.S., and a 28-acre cranberry bog on the reservation is operated by the LCO Cranberry Producers. For general information, call 715-634-8934.

The four annual Lac Courte Oreilles powwows are high points on the reservation. **Sigwan** is held in spring; **Nibin** is a summer celebration; **Datwagi** is the autumn powwow; and **Bibon** is held in winter. The mid-summer Honor the Earth Powwow is the largest, as it provides an opportunity for family reunions on the reservation and is considered a tribal homecoming. Dancing is a featured daily event, and craftspeople from across the country attend. The powwow includes workshops in Ojibwa language and tradition, games, a ten-kilometer road race, plus a regional softball tournament.

The **LCO Bingo Palace and Casino** (Highways K and E on Trepania Road, 715-634-4422 or 715-634-4218) is located outside of Hayward on the reservation. It's open Monday through Thursday and Sunday.

The **Ojibwa Nation Museum** (715-634-8934) documents the history of this Ojibwa band and others, and is located on the reservation.

St. Croix Band

When the Marten Clan left Madeline Island, the travelers found that the upper portion of the St. Croix River was fed by four other rivers: the Clam, the Brule, the Namekagon, and the Yellow. The region was particularly rich. Wild rice grew in abundance, as did birch trees to be used for baskets, canoes, and building. Great flocks of birds, herds of animals, and endless supplies of fish were discovered. Ojibwa settlement of the area began about 300 years after their forefathers landed on the southern shore of Lake Superior.

The fur trade led to prosperity for about a century. One of the first of the villages, called Danbury, was established on Shell Lake. The traders and travelers along the Namekagon Trail called the place "Dogtown" because so many of the residents had dogs. As years passed, the village of Danbury moved, until it was located where the Namekagon River flows into the St. Croix.

During the lumber era, Ojibwa became skilled timbermen, and the St.

Croix was one of the primary logging avenues to the Mississippi. Three other villages were settled, one at Clam Lake, another at Sand Lake, and a third at Bashaw Lake, each of which was rich in wild rice. By 1804, both the British and the French had established trading posts in the region.

Over the next 50 years, a series of treaties were made between the Ojibwa and the U.S. government. The St. Croix people believed that they had lived up to their parts of the agreements, and that they posed no threat to the Great White Father. When the Treaty of 1854 was proposed, redefining tribal boundaries and calling for cession of lands, Chief Yabanse, or "Little Buck," believed that nothing could be achieved by making another long trip to Washington, D.C.

The tribe's absence was duly noted by the federal authorities, and provided the excuse needed to assume complete control over one of Wisconsin's richest forested areas and one of its most abundant waterways to the Mississippi. Thus the St. Croix became the legendary "Lost Tribe of the Ojibwa." For all intents and purposes, they were now landless and homeless. They might work for lumber companies coming into the area, but they could no longer hunt, fish, gather rice, or sugarbush with impunity, as they had done for more than 150 years. As a group, they were forced to move, to separate, and to take up isolated or independent lives. When the logging stopped, so did the timber jobs. Since they were not citizens–Native Americans did not qualify for U.S. citizenship until 1924–few rights were accorded them.

When the 1934 Indian Reorganization Act was passed, the St. Croix at least had an opportunity to borrow funds. With these funds, they bought land, formed their own tribal entity, and made their own laws. Educational and training programs were set in motion. In addition, the St. Croix were recognized as a band of the Ojibwa, and the federal government purchased 1,750 acres for use as a reservation. By World War II, the St. Croix Ojibwa had reorganized themselves and formed their own tribal government.

Today tribal holdings exist in five places: Big Round Lake, the Danbury area of the St. Croix, Clam Lake, Big Sand Lake, and Bashaw Lake. The tribal council operates a store in Danbury and a factory in Siren that builds canoes, while the tribal center is used as a bingo hall. About 2,000 St. Croix live in these settlements. Slowly but surely, they are buying land that has special value to them. In 1980, for example, with the help of the state and federal governments, the St. Croix purchased land called the Altern Mounds, located near Hertel. The mounds were sacred burial sites for people who lived in the area long before the tribe came to St. Croix, and more than 50 mounds are located within the 50-acre tract. For general information about the tribe, call 715-349-2195.

Every year, the St. Croix hold a **Wild Rice Powwow** in Hertel. The tribe has recently joined the Burnett County Historical Society in supporting a replication of a French fort and trading post, **Fort Folles Avoine Historical Park.** During the summer season, St. Croix dancers, drummers, and singers come to

A ceremonial antler headdress, often worn by a chief.

the site and perform for visitors.

St. Croix Tribal Bingo (Highways 8 and 63, 715-986-4161) is located in Turtle Lake, and is open Tuesday, Wednesday, and Friday evenings.

Sokaogon Band of Mole Lake

The chief of the Marten Clan, Kijiwabesheshi or "Great Marten," led a group east along the same trails covered earlier by the Crane Clane. Marten Clan members chose to stay in the area that is now Langlade, Forest, and Oneida counties, specifically by Pickeral, Metonga, White Eye, Mole, Pelican and Post lakes. The last of these lakes contained an unusual stump or wooden post, which was an object of sacred regard for people who lived nearby. The people became known as the *Sokaogon*, or "Post-in-the-Lake People."

The early days of settlement were promising, for the land held much game, many fish, and few enemies. The Sokaogon defended their new territory by driving the Sioux and the Fox away. The last battle between the Sioux and the Sokaogon took place in 1806, when the enemy tried to take away Sokaogon rice fields. Chief Kijiwabesheshi led his warriors against the intruders in what was later known as the Battle of Mole Lake.

Kijiwabesheshi was a statesman among the Ojibwa, and at an 1826 treaty meeting in Fond du Lac, he was given a special peace and friendship medal from President John Quincy Adams. Four years later, however, Andrew Jackson's Indian Removal Act essentially negated all previous treaties. The Ojibwa of Wisconsin traveled to Washington several times to argue their rights, and an 1847 treaty granted the Sokaogon a 12-square-mile area surrounding Mole Lake–signed, sealed, but not delivered. Bureaucrats neglected to give the Sokaogon anything resembling a title to the land.

In 1854 the Sokaogon again traveled to the capital to agree to a treaty, but by the time it was officially signed on Madeline Island, the Sokaogon portion had mysteriously vanished. According to one story, the bureaucrat carrying the treaty back to Washington drowned when his ship went down, and the treaty went down with him. Someone then contrived to steal the Sokaogon chief's copy, and the map or deed was lost as well.

For eight decades, the Sokaogon had no official record of their participation in the treaty, nor record of the parcel of land specified for their reservation. It was a difficult time for the people. In 1934, with the passage of the Indian Reorganization Act, the Sokaogon were finally allotted a place they could call their own. They were quick to form their own governmental body, based on a constitution of their own making, and to govern themselves through their own legal structure. What they received in 1934, however, in no way resembles the 12 square miles promised them almost a century earlier.

Today the Sokaogon Ojibwa reside on 1,680 acres. There are no lakes within the small area, and one must drive a mile or so outside of the Mole Lake Reservation in order to find Mole Lake. About 500 people live on the reservation, one-third of which are school-age children. Of the estimated 225 members of employment age, only about 40 percent have jobs. For general information about the band or its reservation, call 715-478-2604.

Mole Lake Tribal Bingo (715-478-2604) in Crandon is a major source of income for the tribe. The hall is open Tuesdays, Fridays, Saturdays, and Sundays. The tribe shares the site with Potawatomi neighbors who operate the **Forest County Potawatomi Bingo** on Monday, Wednesday, and Thursday evenings.

Potawatomi

Along with the Ojibwa and the Ottawa, the Potawatomi were part of the Anishinabe people, whose original tribal homeland was on the gulf of the St. Lawrence River. Therefore, the Potawatomi heritage includes the Megis Shell migration west hundreds of years ago. As the three groups divided to determine their own destinies, those called the *Bodewadmi*, or Potawatomi, were

A traditional, costumed corn husk doll

the designated "keepers of the sacred flame." They settled in the area known as Bawating–today's Sault Ste. Marie–and a number moved to Michigan's Upper Peninsula and later into Wisconsin.

The Potawatomi built their domed dwellings, called wigwams, in various areas according to seasonal resources and traditional hunting, fishing, or harvesting practices. Summers found them in places where they could farm; winter moved them to sheltered valleys; and spring took them south to hunt larger game, including buffalo. By 1641, the Potawatomi had moved out of Michigan as a result of a conflict with another tribe. They settled in Wisconsin–especially in the area known today as Door County, including Washington Island.

French traders found the Potawatomi hospitable and eager traders. The people began to move further south as the tribe itself grew in numbers. By 1800, they were living as far south as the shores of the Mississippi River in Illinois. More than 50 Potawatomi villages were located in the states of Wisconsin, Illinois, Michigan, and Indiana. Their relationship with the French led them to join the Europeans in battles with the Iroquois, the Fox, and the Mascouten, and they themselves fought the Winnebago. The tribe also sided with the French against the English in the French and Indian War.

By the time of the Revolutionary War, peace had been made with the English, so the Potawatomi chose to support that side in the war for colonial independence. Even in the War of 1812, the Potawatomi maintained their alliance with the English. Under Presidents Monroe and Jackson, the Potawatomi, like most Native American nations, were forced to move or to renegotiate treaties in court. Under terms of the Treaty of Chicago in 1833, the Potawatomi ceded five million acres to the U.S. government.

By 1836 the Potawatomi had been moved to two reservations far from their homelands, one in Kansas and the other in Iowa. Ten years later these were combined to form one reservation in Kansas. Some among the Potawatomi, however, refused to go. If forced to leave, they would escape and return to the areas they had held for many years. Some hid in the forests of Wisconsin, while others emigrated to Canada. In 1868, some of those on the Kansas reservation were moved to a smaller site in Oklahoma.

By 1894 a fairly significant number of families had established residence in Wisconsin's Forest County. At the turn of the century, 30 Potawatomi families lived in the county and 450 tribespeople lived elsewhere in Wisconsin or in nearby northern Michigan. The federal government continued to try to get the Potawatomi to move to Kansas or Oklahoma, but the people refused.

The resisting residents reminded the federal government that a number of unfulfilled promises had been made under the Treaty of Chicago and other agreements. The Potawatomi petitioned for payments owed them. The government finally agreed, but told the Potawatomi that cash payments were not viable; land would be the currency used. Payments of four kinds would be made to the Wisconsin Potawatomi: land, homes, improvements, and farming equipment.

No reservation was assigned to them, however, so the Wisconsin Potawatomi began buying scattered pieces of land in Forest County. They were not entitled to live together as a tribal entity, but in 1934 the Indian Reorganization Act allowed them to create a tribal government and make laws.

Today, though there is no specific Forest County Potawatomi reservation, about 11,000 acres are owned by tribal members. Two communities–Wabeno and Stone Lake–are considered tribal settlements. Over $600,000 promised in 1921 by the federal government was only recently paid to the tribe, and it's hoped that this money will allow them to purchase more land.

The two communities constitute the general constituency for the tribal council, and meetings are held at the tribal center in Stone Lake. The nearly 500 people living in the county are struggling to maintain the Potawatomi language and religion. Although some Potawatomi work as guides for non-Indian hunters and fishermen, no specific tourist industry exists for the Forest County residents, who are plagued by an unemployment rate nearing 80 percent of the employable persons. For general information about the tribe, call 715-479-2903.

A pair of child's moccasins, crafted by the Potawatomi.

141

Forest County Potawatomi Bingo (715-478-2604) in Crandon is held on Monday, Wednesday, and Thursday evenings. **Potawatomi Bingo** (1721 W. Canal St., 800-755-6171 or 414-645-6888) operates in Milwaukee; proceeds are dedicated to the Indian Community School and other community services.

Oneida

The newest Native American residents in the state are the Oneida and the Stockbridge-Munsee. Both migrated from the east. The Oneida left the Iroquois Confederacy in the first decades of the 19th century to follow a religious leader west, while the Stockbridge-Munsee are Mohicans who also came at the inspiration of a charismatic person and negotiated for themselves a small portion of land held by the Menominee.

The Oneida were part of the Iroquois Confederacy, which also included the Mohawks, Onondagas, Cayugas, and the Senecas, for many years. This confederation remains remarkable for its achievements, and for its demonstration that nations can work together to solve both individual and common problems.

The Iroquois Confederacy met on a regular basis. Each tribe sent its

An Oneida longhouse, protected by a section of stockade.

representatives to sit in council meetings, and each tribal clan–the wolf, the turtle, the bear–was represented. The leaders were called *sachems*, and clan mothers chose these leaders. In fact, the confederacy was a matriarchal society, for the women of each nation not only selected *sachems*, but also controlled land usage, child-rearing, and the election of chiefs.

The Iroquois were not a migratory people. They moved villages according to the environment's ability to sustain each nation or community. Labor and tribal responsibilities were divided according to the needs of the people. They were called "Longhouse Indians" because of the great log structures they built for religious, health, political, and domestic purposes. Some were as long as 150 feet. Some were built like apartments, with space allocated for families or functions. In an Iroquois village, longhouses of all kinds were constructed within a wall of upended logs that protected residents from human or animal intruders.

During the French and Indian War in the early 18th century, the confederacy faced its first divisive situation. The Oneidas chose to fight on the side of the English, while most others in the confederation backed the French. With the English victory, a rift was created, and this was enlarged before the American Revolution when a colonial missionary, Samuel Kirkland, proposed

The interior of an Oneida longhouse, replete with log bunks.

that tribal government be reorganized. Later, pro-English Oneida took sides against pro-American Oneidas in the Revolutionary War.

At war's end, the Oneida found their longhouses destroyed and their fields laid to waste. The tribe was scattered from Schenectady to Niagara Falls. A treaty in 1784 attempted to re-establish land claims, but the state of New York wanted the land for non-Indian interests. For 60 years, the Oneida struggled against the state, attempting to retain their territorial rights. The fact that other members of the confederacy maintained a certain resentment of the Oneida did not help, but they, too, were fighting for their proprietary rights.

Another generation of missionaries entered the scene. In 1820, one Eleazer Williams led a band of Oneida followers to Wisconsin. The decision to leave was not an easy one–nor was it an easy journey. When the group arrived, they discovered that the land they had hoped to settle belonged to the Menominee. Diplomatic negotiations and Menominee generosity provided the Oneida with about four million acres along the Fox River and near present-day Oneida, Wisconsin. The good fortune was short-lived, however, as the Andrew Jackson policy of Indian removal and aggressive non-Indian timber interests

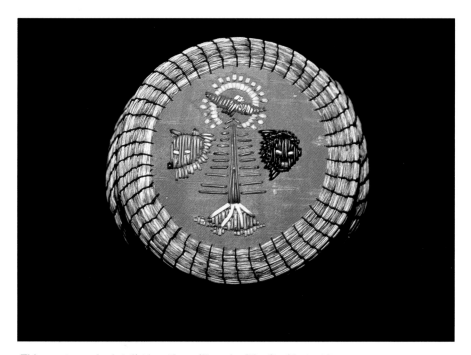

This sweetgrass basket displays the quill work of the Oneida people.

quickly whittled down the territory.

By 1887, with the passage of the Dawes Allotment Act, each Oneida was permitted to hold only 26 acres. This again divided the tribe, for individuals were recognized, not families. As a result, many families were split and members were sent to different parts of the area. Today the Oneida reservation contains only 2,800 acres.

Oneida now living on the reservation number about 5,000, with another 5,000 enrolled Oneida living elsewhere. Relations with the Iroquois Confederacy have been maintained over the years. The Oneida tribal government was established in 1937, and the official body, called the Oneida Business Committee, is composed of nine members including the chairman.

Tribal government provides education for Oneida youth, and a Headstart Program has been implemented on the reservation, as have career training programs. The Oneida maintain and manage a health care facility for seniors, but clinical services are provided to tribal members, too. A number of community health programs are provided through the tribal center, including nutrition courses, drug and alcohol treatment and counseling, child care, and

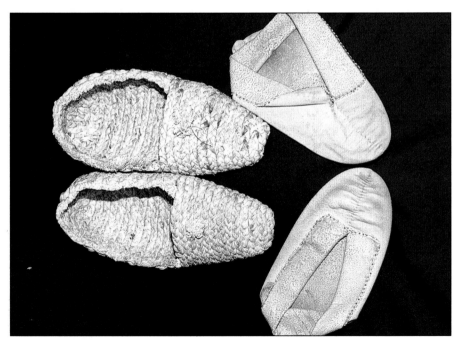

Oneida moccasins

physical fitness.

The Oneida language, Iroquois, is taught in the schools. The Native American Church retains a small following, but the majority of members belong to the Catholic or Protestant churches located on the reservation. The Iroquois have long been noted for their quill work and bead artistry, and some craft items created by the Oneida are sold to the public. Most traditional crafts, though, are used for clothing and other accoutrements in ceremonies and powwow dancing. For general information, call 414-569-1260.

The Oneida culture is well represented by the **Oneida Nation Museum** (414-869-2768) in Oneida, considered by many to be the most complete display found on a Wisconsin reservation. The museum's primary purpose is to teach younger Oneida about their past and about the origins of many traditions valued within the Iroquois heritage. However, it was also created to educate non-Indian visitors. The museum is built on one of the last parcels of the original reservation land grant.

The Iroquois Confederacy was regarded by many colonial Americans, including Ben Franklin, as a model form of representational government. A number of historians have traced portions of the Articles of Confederation and the Constitution to the time-held practices of the Confederacy's Great Council. Therefore, a significant part of the Oneida museum's collection is the series of wampum belts, including the legendary "George Washington Belt" given to the tribe during Washington's term as the nation's first president. The six-foot wampum belt represents a peace treaty between the thirteen new states and the Iroquois Confederacy, symbolized by two figures that represent the Mohawks and the Senecas. These groups were, respectively, the keepers of the confederacy's eastern and western doors.

The annual **Oneida Nation Powwow** on July 4 serves as a tribal ceremony and concludes the yearly election of council members and the tribal chairman. The powwow is held at the Norbert Hill Tribal Center in Oneida.

The Oneida own and manage **First American Games** (800-238-4263 or 414-497-8118), one of the country's most successful bingo halls. It's open seven days a week, games are played twice each day, and the hall has a capacity of 1,000 persons. It's located next door to the 200-room Radisson Hotel (414-494-7300 or 800-333-3333), another Oneida enterprise. The reservation is located near the city limits of Green Bay, and numerous accommodations, restaurants, and other attractions are available.

The Oneida maintain a number of additional business interests, including convenience stores, a tribal farm, and the **Oneida Community Cannery** (414-869-4377), which processes fruits, vegetables, wild game and traditional Iroquois foods. Cannery items are sold to members and to the general public. There is a tribal printing enterprise and an Oneida Research and Technology

A modern corn husk doll created by the Oneida.

Center, also called ORTEK. The tribe intends to repurchase as much of the original holdings as possible, so the Oneida own significant real estate tracts in the Green Bay and DePere area.

Stockbridge-Munsee

Each of the Native American nations in Wisconsin has its own unique history and heritage, but the people called Stockbridge-Munsee might be considered the most historically fascinating. Originally, the people were members of two distinct national groups, the Mahicans and the Munsee. The Mahicans were also known as the Housatonic Indians, the River Indians, or the *Mu-he-con-neok* when they lived in the eastern portion of the continent. The Munsee were a band of the Delawares, belonging to another eastern nation. The two were compatible, and intermingled over centuries as they lived in the same area.

It can be said that the Mahicans are the only Native Americans in Wisconsin whose origin can be aligned with the "land bridge" theory, which suggests that the first continental inhabitants came across the Bering Straits when the Asian and American continents were close enough to permit an easy crossing.

According to Mahican legend, a great people came from the northwest, crossing waters where lands nearly touched each other. A great period of wandering is remembered as the people searched for the ideal homeland, and many settlements were established along the way. The people were searching for a place where the waters were never still. They finally reached the eastern ocean coast, and here they divided into different tribes.

The oldest of the tribes was the *Mu-he-con-neok*, which lived along the *Muhheakunnuk*, now called the Hudson River. The currents of the river, as well as the tidal changes that took place near the sea, convinced the Mahicans that this was the place where waters never ceased moving. Centuries passed before Europeans arrived at the river's mouth or at coastal harbors. The Mahicans' territory extended upriver, and into present-day Vermont.

The Munsee found their own never-still waters along the Delaware River basin. Part of their territory butted against the shores of the Hudson, thus creating a linkage between the two groups.

The lifestyles, dress, and building methods of the two groups were quite similar, so when a merger came later, it came without hostility. The area in which they lived was filled with forests and fields, rivers and streams, animals and fish. Plentiful wood was available for the building of longhouses, which were combined to create a village or community. As many as 200 people would live in these enclaves. Every decade or so, the entire village would pack up and move to another location, as resources were depleted and the

The Radisson-Green Bay Hotel, owned by the Oneida tribe.

environment needed time to restore itself. The men were hunters and fishermen, while the women were the farmers and gardeners. The clothing–Munsee or Mahican–was made mainly of skins, decorated with shells or beads. Later, when European traders came with goods and materials, styles were adapted to utilize new ingredients such as silk, broadcloth, and linen or wool. Appliques became fashionable, as did velvet collars for women's blouses and brass and silver buttons.

In the early 17th century, European traders created a climate of competition among the Native American nations, a climate that often led tribes to warfare in attempts to win a "market share." Caught in this industrial conflict were the Mahicans, who were pitted against the Mohawks for control of the Hudson River fur trade. The Mahicans lost. As a result, they were forced to move from their beloved valley, away from the waters that were never still. They looked for another location that might offer some of the same features, and settled in what is now the Connecticut River valley. The competition for furs continued, however, and conflicts multiplied. Relocations became a way of life.

To complicate things further for the Mahicans, Christianity entered the

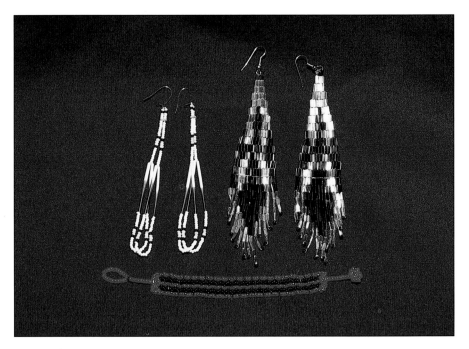

Modern Oneida beadwork

scene. John Sergeant chose to live with the Mahicans, to convert the people of western Massachusetts. He baptized people, changed their names, preached to them. In 1738, Sergeant was given permission to create a mission village called Stockbridge. Since both Mahicans and Munsee lived nearby, both were soon being called Stockbridge Indians. A number of of the Munsee, however, migrated north to Canada.

During the Revolutionary War, the Mahicans and the Munsees fought on the side of the colonials. Their losses were exceptionally high. It's estimated that half of the population of the two tribes was lost in the fighting. Further devastation to the eastern tribal nations was caused by diseases imported from Europe.

Assumption of statehood by the thirteen colonies increased the number of non-Indian settlements and encouraged migration westward. Stockbridge itself was relocated due to population changes. New Stockbridge was located across the border, in New York. The Stockbridge, as they were known by then, adapted by becoming farmers, spinning wool and making baskets, and cutting timber.

A carved cedar flute

New Stockbridge was in the midst of a fertile area with rich soil and fine forests. Soon, New York's government moved to increase development for its citizens, which did not include the Stockbridge tribe. In 1818, a small band of Stockbridge accepted an offer by the Delaware and Miami nations to share land in Indiana. When they arrived, they learned that the land had been sold to non-Indian developers.

At the time, Native American affairs were being handled by the federal government's War Department. The government arranged in 1822 to buy land from the Winnebago and Menominee nations in Wisconsin, in order to provide space for the Stockbridge along the Fox River, where the present-day Kaukauna is located. An additional 225 Stockbridge, joined by 100 Delaware and Munsee, moved to this area in 1831. The 1830s were times of turmoil among the people. There were quarrels over the land. The Munsee who had gone to Canada now returned and moved into Wisconsin. And the Jackson Indian Removal Act of 1830 had dramatic implications for virtually all nations.

A number of the Stockbridge grew tired of the negotiations and relocations, and chose to move on to the Missouri, Kansas, and Oklahoma territories. Their journeys were long and arduous. Many died, and many returned to their "home" in Wisconsin. Between 1843 and 1856, the people argued that they be allowed to remain in Wisconsin. Finally, in 1856, the Stockbridge and their friends the Munsee were given land east of Lake Winnebago. They were also joined, at the time, by a small group of Brotherton Indians and by Iroquois from New York.

For the rest of the 19th century, the multi-national group fought to keep its land and to retain something of its heritage. Land was lost under terms of the General Allotment Act, which held that some reservation land was not tribally owned and could be sold by individuals. As economic conditions worsened, more land was sold to make ends meet.

With the 1934 Indian Reorganization Act, the Stockbridge-Munsee, as they were now called, were allowed to try to recover some of the lost territory. Four years later, the tribe had 2,250 acres to call homeland–a small area set on the lower southwestern border of the Menominee Reservation. It wasn't much, but for the people it was a beginning of growing back together again.

Unfortunately the relocations, the multiplicity of cultures contained within the "tribe," and economic difficulties had affected the retention of Native American heritage. Languages were lost, customs were not carried on, arts and crafts were neglected. The reservation lost its school, so children were taken to nearby towns where non-Indians were a decisive majority. Men and some women left the reservation to find employment that would sustain their families; entire families often left.

One cultural tradition continued, however. At some point in their history, the Stockbridge-Munsee people began to pile rocks wherever they lived. Some believe it was a way of marking one's home, while others consider it

A carved frog decoy and fishing spear.

paying homage to Mother Earth. According to one story, when hunters would leave the village for long periods in the old days, they would bring back a stone. The stone would be placed on an existing pile, marking the boundary for that particular village. According to another version, stone-piling was a way of recognizing the death of a chief–a burial mound made of stone. In Stockbridge, Massachusetts, a Monument Mountain exists, made of stones. There is another in Wisconsin.

A "contemporary custom" with traditional roots emerged in 1965. At that time Edwin Martin, a Mahican, created a design representing a walking stick, the marvelous insect that looks like a four-legged twig. One day someone tried to remember what the creature was called, asking, "Where can I find the 'Many Trails' design?" After considerable discussion, it was determined that the person was referring to "Walking Stick." The notion of "Many Trails" caught on, and it was soon being used to adorn t-shirts, rings, necklaces, belt buckles, and works of art. Accidentally, the Stockbridge-Munsee had discovered a new symbol for their determination to survive and to thrive as a united people. At the center of the design is a turtle, which has traditionally been sacred to many Woodland Indians, including the Mahicans.

Today, about 500 Stockbridge-Munsee live on the 11,692-acre reservation. A recent initiative taken by the state of Wisconsin, designating the reservation

Students learn from tribal members at the Milwaukee Indian Community School.

as an economic development zone, may change the nearly 80 percent unemployment of the existing tribal labor force. For general information about the tribe, call 715-793-4111.

The **Mohican Bingo Hall** (County Trunk K, Rt. 2, 800-922-8442) in Bowler brings income to the reservation to assist in development. It's open Wednesday through Sunday, and a "Motel Stay and Play Package" (800-752–0063) is available.

Work has been completed on a reservation campground. The camping area has been called "one of the state's most beautiful undiscovered areas," and it's being adapted to accommodate winter camping and cross country ski trails. Plans have been made to build a traditional village, which will enable visitors to live according to Mahican and Munsee traditions.

The **Stockbridge-Munsee Historical Library and Museum** (Mohheconnuck Road, 715-793-4270) in Bowler offers historical books, papers, artifacts, and exhibits. A recent acquisition was a two-volume Bible originally given to the Stockbridge-Munsee tribe in 1745 by the pastor to the Prince of Wales. Craft items are offered for sale here, as well.

A health fair, sponsored by Milwaukee's Indian Health Center.

Publications

In addition to **News From Indian Country,** a national newspaper published by the Lac Courte Oreilles Ojibwa, a number of Native American papers are published in Wisconsin. These include:

ZOAR's Weekly Information, 5722 North 43rd St., Milwaukee, 53209

Native American Council, 204 Student Center, University of Wisconsin, River Falls 54022

Menominee Tribal News, P.O. Box 397, Keshena 54135

Menominee Indian News, Neopit 54150

KALIHWISAKS, P.O.Box 98, Oneida 54155

Shenandoah News, 736 West Oklahoma St., Appleton 54911

Stockbridge-Munsee Newsletter, Rt. 1, Bowler 54416

Winnebago News, Rt. 1, Creamery Rd., Nekoosa 54457

Smoke Signals, Rt. 2, Box 400, Odanah 54806

Lac du Flambeau Update, LDF Tribal Office, Lac du Flambeau 54538

Powwows and Events

The annual **Indian Summer Festival** (414-383-7425) that takes place in Milwaukee during early September is Wisconsin's largest powwow. At about the same time the Red Cliff Ojibwa hold their **Traditional Powwow** (715-779-5805) on the Red Cliff Reservation outside Bayfield. Other annual powwows not mentioned elsewhere include the Lac du Flambeau Ojibwa's **Bear River Powwow** (715-588-3346), held on the reservation in mid-July; the **Oneida Festival of the Performing Arts** (414-869-1260 or 414-869-2083), held at St. Norbert's College in the first week of July; the **Land of the Menominee Powwow** (715-799-4423), held in Keshena in early August; and about one week later, **Stockbridge-Munsee Indian Powwow** (715-793-4111) in Bowler.

Two prehistoric Native American eras are celebrated in Wisconsin, as well. In early June, Oconto holds its **Old Copper Culture Festival** (414-834-5136) at the nearby state park, honoring the heritage of the town and the park. **Aztalan Day** is held in Lake Mills during the first week of July, and this event focuses upon the heritage of the nearby park and the Aztalan Museum. It's sponsored by the Lake Mills-Aztalan Historical Society (414-648-5085).

In July and August, Lac du Flambeau Ojibwa hold their annual **Wisconsin Native American Artist Show** (715-588-3346) in downtown Lac du Flambeau. On Madeline Island in mid-August, **Ojibwa Craft Day** (715-747-2415) is devoted to the work of traditional and contemporary Ojibwa artisans. During the first week in September, Oshkosh holds the annual **E.K. Petrie Indian Artifact Show**, which has been going on for more than six decades. Visitors come from all around the nation to sell, swap, and shop for Native American artifacts; special activities, historical encampments, and re-enactments are also offered on the grounds of the **Oshkosh Public Museum** (1331 Algoma Blvd., 414-236-5150).

Historical Sites

Fort Folles Avoine (715-866-8890), a reconstruction of the French fort and trading post built long ago on the site, is located near Webster. This is a co-operative venture between the St. Croix Ojibwa people and the Burnett County Historical Society. Near Wauzeka, travelers will find the **Kickapoo Indian Caverns and Native American Museum** (Highway 60, 608-875-5223). The cave was a longtime shelter for various Indian peoples, and there are guided tours to the natural historic site. A trading post is also located on the premises. In Portage, the **1832 Old Indian Agency House** (Agency House Rd., 608-742-6362) was built for John Kinzie and his wife, Juliette, who would later write the classic frontier account, *Wau-Bun*. The house sits opposite the site of Fort Winnebago, and faces the canal built near the old portage between the Fox and Wisconsin rivers. It's open to the public for an admission fee from May through October, and by appointment during the winter months.

Museums

Numerous museums in Wisconsin either specialize in Native American collections or offer significant exhibits relating to Indian life in the state. There are six museums and cultural centers on reservations, and these will be highlighted in sections to follow. However, non-affiliated museums also exist and are open to the public.

Beloit College's **Logan Museum of Anthropology** (608-365-3391) in Beloit contains an extensive collection of North American Indian exhibits, including materials from Great Lakes Indians as well as the Plains and Southwest Indians; there is a special collection of Arikara archaeology, and the "Albert Green Heath Collection of Native American Artifacts."

The **Chippewa Valley Museum** in Eau Claire's Carson Park offers a collection of artifacts and photographs of Ojibwa, Menominee, and Winnebago people, as well as a library.

In the Door County community of Egg Harbor, the **Chief Oshkosh Museum** (7631 Egg Harbor Rd., 414-868-3240) includes a collection of the personal possessions of the chief of the Menominees, as well as exhibits of the artifacts and craftwork of other Native American tribes. The museum is open from May until October.

In Hayward, **Historyland** is designed to promote Native American self-awareness and perpetuate their cultural contributions to the arts. Collections here showcase the work of Ojibwa artists, and crafts by Ojibwa artisans. For information contact the Hayward Chamber of Commerce at 715-634-8662 or 800-826-3474.

In Madison, the **Museum of the State Historical Society** contains both an exhibit facility (30 North Carroll St.) and a collections library (816 State St.). Exhibits display Woodland and Plains Indians artifacts, as well as prehistoric archaeological discoveries. A number of special collections include the H.P. Hamilton Collection of Copper Culture artifacts; the Titus Collection of Southwest Indian pottery; and the Draper Manuscript Collection, named after the Society's first secretary, which contains the works of Henry R. Schoolcraft, the first Indian agent appointed to the Wisconsin Territory. The Historical Society also offers special classes, shows films, and owns audiotape and photographic collections dealing with Native American cultural life.

In Manitowoc, the **Rahr Public Museum** (610 North 8th St.) has a collection of artifacts that were gathered within Manitowoc County, including Copper Culture materials.

The **Milwaukee Public Museum** (800 West Wells St., 414-278-2752) includes more than 20,000 specimens and artifacts collected throughout North America. The museum houses a number of dioramas, and sponors school tours of various Native American areas. It also publishes books, among them *North American Indian Lives*, *Building a Chippewa Indian Canoe*, and *Indians of Wisconsin*, and a quarterly museum publication is entitled *Lore*. The museum library contains 125,000 monographs and periodicals on natural and human history, as well as over 300,000 photographs, with particular strength in the depiction of American Indian life.

In Sheboygan, the **John Michael Kohler Arts Center** (608 New York Ave., 414-458-6144) has more than 5,000 artifacts in its collection, including pottery, weapons, axes and other tools, and copper implements. Library facilities there are available only to researchers.

The **Fairlawn Historical Museum** in Superior (906 East 2nd. St., 715-394-5712) includes the David F. Barry collection of Sioux portraits, as well as the George Catlin lithographs of the Plains Indians. Catlin's work is particularly distinguished, preserving many aspects of Indian life and culture. The museum also includes artifacts and a library.

The **Waukesha County Historical Museum** (101 West Main St., 414-544-8430) in Waukesha is located on the Mound of the Turtle. It contains artifacts taken from that earthwork.

The **Hoard Historical Museum Library** (407 Merchant Ave.) in Fort Atkinson maintains a special collection of rare books written about Black Hawk and the Black Hawk War, spanning the years 1800 to 1840.

Native American Centers

Most of the Native American Centers in Wisconsin are oriented toward improved health care and health services. In Green Bay, centers and organizations include the **United AmerIndian Health Center** (414-435-6773), and the **American Indian Council on Alcoholism** (2240 West National Ave.).

The **Milwaukee Indian Urban Affairs Council** shares its location with the **Milwaukee Indian Health Board and Center** (930 North 27th St.). For information, call the Urban Affairs office at 414-342-4171 and the Health Board at 414-931-8111.

The **Native American Center** (UW-Stevens Point, 715-346-3828) of Stevens Point serves as a resource center for Native American history and culture, especially pertaining to Wisconsin and the Upper Midwest. The center also sponsors outreach programs, assists in adult education programs, promotes inter-cultural activities, and sponsors an annual powwow on the university campus.

Courses of Study

The **University of Wisconsin-Madison** offers an American Indian Studies Program (1188 Education Science Bldg., 1025 West Johnson St., 608-263-5501), which includes graduate and undergraduate counseling, course offerings, special lectures, and an annual powwow. The program recruits faculty to provide curricula meaningful to both Indians and non-Indians.

The **University of Wisconsin-Milwaukee** (414-229-1122) also includes a Native American Studies Program within its College of Letters and Sciences. Course offerings range from Great Lakes Indian ethnobotany to anthropology and ethnology, history and philosophy, and dreams and visions in American Indian metaphysics. The program holds an annual art festival and sponsors the **Wisconsin Woodland American Indian Summer Field Institute**.

Marquette University (414-288-6838) in Milwaukee offers Native American courses in its Social and Cultural Sciences Department, and has a special program called **American Indian Counsellor**. The university sponsors an annual powwow, and its library houses the archives of the Catholic Board of Indian Missions.

In Ashland, **Northland College** (1411 Ellis Ave.) has a Native American Studies Department that provides a range of courses for Indian and non-Indian students.

The **Lac Courte Oreilles Ojibwa Community College** in Hayward (715-634-4790) offers a two-year course of study that includes a range of Native American language, literature, and history courses.

Medicine Rock, near Lac du Flambeau.

Native Wisconsin

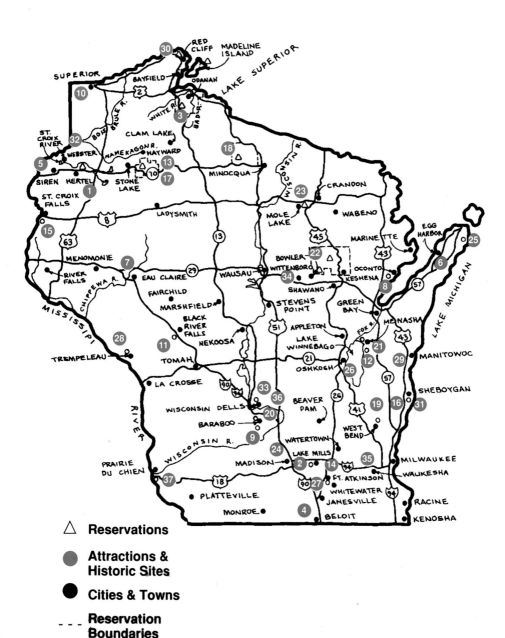

△ **Reservations**

● **Attractions & Historic Sites**

● **Cities & Towns**

- - - **Reservation Boundaries**

7

Minnesota: Sky on Water

Minnesota takes its name from the Sioux, the key element being *minne* or "water." The most poetic English interpretation of the name is "reflection of sky on water."

Once the great Wisconsin Glacier had departed, leaving behind Minnesota's famed 10,000 lakes, the Sioux people's description became definitive, at least in the lakeland region of the state. A line can be drawn, however, at about the valley of the Minnesota River, making this the northeastern corner of the Great Plains Basin. From a geological point of view this is interesting; from an ethnological perspective, it's critical to an understanding of what separated the Woodlands Indians from the Plains Indians, for their lifestyles and cultures were very different, and were defined by their environments. What makes comparisons intriguing is that many of the Native Americans who would consider the plains their homeland crossed the Woodlands Indians' Minnesota environment on their way to the plains.

Ancient Times

There is limited archaeological evidence of Paleo-Indian or Archaic Indian habitation in what is now Minnesota.

Near International Falls, there is **Grand Mound** and the **Grand Mound History Center** (Hwy 11, 218-279-3332), which is considered the largest prehistoric mound in Minnesota and is maintained by the Minnesota Historical Society. The Interpretive Center provides background on the "Laurel" Indians, who lived in the area from 200 B.C. until about 800 A.D. An exhibit is offered, and the center contains self-guided hiking trails. The site is open from Memorial Day until Labor Day.

One of Minnesota's most fascinating "natural" museums is found outdoors. The **Jeffers Petroglyphs** (Hwy 71 and Cty Rd 45, 507-877-3647 or 507-678-2331) are situated just outside Bingham Lake. Here, more than 2,000 etchings are visible on red sandstone outcroppings that date back more than 4,000 years, with some extending into post-European times. The petroglyphs show carvings of humans, animals, tools, weapons, and other designs. An exhibit relates various interpretations of the drawings. The site is open from Memorial Day until Labor Day.

Kathio State Park (Highway 169) near Onamia has an interpretive center that describes the archaeological aspects of the park, including mounds and

Winnewissa Falls, near Pipestone National Monument

villages. Some of the ongoing digs in the park are open to the public.

In St. Paul, **Mounds Park** (Mounds Blvd. and East Sixth St.) contains six mounds–about one-third of the estimated number that once stood on this site.

Migrations

While the Algonquians were living in the northeastern part of present-day Minnesota, the rest of the region belonged to the Sioux, who were largely living on the Great Plains. Maps in the *Atlas of the North American Indian* trace different nations as they migrated into the Great Plains.

Evidence indicates that many tribal groups lived throughout this area for centuries, traveling south during the glacial epoch at times when warming trends created relatively safe passageways. Some experts have determined that in the 1200s, a great drought covered the plains from Canada to Mexico, probably similar to the desert-making drought of the 1920s and 1930s in the same area. In both cases, people either left the area or died, for the resources were depleted.

Some people, like the non-agrarian Algonquian Blackfeet, moved north. Others, like the Mandan, the Cado, the Pawnee, and the Wichita, headed south. The drought lasted for quite some time, and it took perhaps another 100 years for the land to refurbish itself with the natural bounty of flora and fauna. As the land regained its fertility, a number of peoples became interested in leaving the colder northern climes of what is now Canada or the northeast

Native Americans in the Great Lakes region use canoes in gathering wild rice.
The stalks are beaten with a stick in order to free the rice kernels.

U.S. for the wide open spaces of the Great Plains.

Minnesota was one of the migratory paths taken by many of these Native American nations, among them the Algonquian Plains Indians. These would include bands of the Sauk and Fox, who chose to roam west of the Mississippi. There were emigrations by peoples who had lived north of the Great Lakes: the Cheyenne, Arapaho, Crow, and others. Siouan bands such as the Assiniboine also played territorial leapfrog over the course of generations, always moving westward.

These were not impractical decisions arising from panic. The grass was, literally, greener and greater across the Mississippi River. Agricultural people who were hunter-gatherers did not find the wide open spaces inhospitable, although one can imagine that it might take time to adjust to a broad, treeless horizon after living in dense forests.

The Gift of Mobility

The Great Plains became the great provider, and cultures adapted to the environment. There were immense herds of game–buffalo, deer, antelope. There were marvelous coveys of gamebirds. Where there were streams, there were fish. And the prairie yielded its own special fruits and vegetables. To the migratory nations that moved according to the seasons of their harvests, this land seemed as endless as the distance beyond the setting sun. The expanse of territory seemed adequate for all nations that might choose the prairies and

Much work is required to separate the wild rice kernels from chaff.

mountains as their homeland. And to this sense of fundamental security--there were always traditional enemies, both natural and human--was added one significant gift from Europeans: the horse.

Horses wandered the continent in its earliest days, but these were small creatures not unlike today's dalmatian or short-hair pointer. And they vanished in the mystery of extinction many centuries before the earliest American Indians became the dominant hemispheric population. The coming of the Spanish, then the French, and finally the English, brought the Europeans' favorite military and exploratory beast of burden to these shores.

It's an understatement to observe that the horse--especially for the Plains Indians--was a significant gift. For the people of the prairies and western mountains, the horse became a sacred addition to the culture, not unlike fire or the buffalo--greater, even, than the introduction of flint, powder, and guns. The horse meant mobility, distance, speed, and the ability to keep up with the buffalo when the time came for the hunt.

People who had been farmers tied to the soil, hunters caught in the seasonal webs of game migration, or fishermen dependent on running waters now had the power of the horse to hunt, to move their families quickly when threatened, to haul possessions that symbolized strength and wealth. The horse became for many of the Plains Indians even more valuable than the beaver, the muskrat, and other furbearing animals were to the fur-trading Woodland Indians.

Incidentally, experts believe that the horse did not reach what is now Minnesota until the time of the Revolutionary War. But in the northern regions by Lake Superior, the horse did not have the value of a canoe. And no one had to feed a canoe in the forest.

The Coming of the French

The French found Lake Superior in about 1660, long after the Ojibwa considered it *Gitchi Gamig*, or the great sacred waters. Among the most admirable and tolerant of explorers were Pierre Esprit Radisson and his partner, Sieur des Groseilliers, who visited the area in 1668. Later came Father Claude Jean Allouez. In 1678 and 1679, Daniel Greysolon, also known as Sieur Du Lhut, traveled west across the Great Lakes to negotiate for the release of fellow French explorers Hennepin and Aco, dealing with both Sioux and Ojibwa. In 1689, Nicolas Perrot claimed the upper reaches of the Mississippi for "New France." And in 1700, Pierre Charles le Sueur entered the region to talk with the Sioux, the Oto, and the Iowa peoples, only to have his small fort attacked by Fox enemies.

Other forts were soon built by the French, to protect their traders and often to protect the Jesuit missionaries who were proselytizing among tribes

Grand Portage National Monument

that were not always receptive to a change in spiritual ideas. From 1727 to the 1750s, the French built Fort Beauharnois in an attempt to stop the Mesquakie Wars, then Fort St. Charles and Fort St. Pierre. Trading posts were built as far west as Rainy Lake and Lake of the Woods.

Historical Attractions

A number of historical attractions in Minnesota portray this important, primary contact with early Europeans.

In Grand Marais, travelers can visit the **Grand Portage National Monument** (Highway 61, 800-232-1384 or 218-387-2788), which includes a reconstructed version of the headquarters for the fur-trading North West Company. The complex also includes a display of Native American artifacts, and there are nine miles of trails within the park. It's open from May until October.

In Ely, the **Vermilion Interpretive Center** (Vermilion Campus, 1900 East Camp St., 218-365-3226) includes artifacts and displays portraying the Ojibwa and French fur traders. An admission fee is charged.

Another **North West Company** fur trading post (Cty Rd 7 and State Route 2, 612-629-6356) is located in Pine City. This one is a reconstruction of a "winter trading post" from the late 1700s, complete with its inventory of goods. The post is open from Memorial Day to Labor Day.

Conflicts and Competition

While intermittent, deadly fighting took place between tribes, the development of the French fur trade created economic competition for territory. When the French established a connection with the Cree, the Mesquakie objected. Meanwhile, a conflict emerged between the Woodland-Algonquian Ojibwa and the Plains-Siouan Dakota.

Several Siouan cultures were significant in the Great Plains. One should note that the word "Sioux" was a French corruption of the Ojibwa term *nadouessioux*, meaning "enemy" or a poisonous snake, the adder. Some tribes spoke languages with a Siouan base, such as the Winnebago of Wisconsin. However, there were four dominant Sioux nations–the Lakota, the Dakota-Santee, the Nakota-Yankton, and the Yanktonai, each of which included several bands. The terms Dakota, Nakota, and Lakota all mean "allies." The Santee would play a distinctive role in the development of historic events and places within the state of Minnesota.

When the French were building forts and establishing their trading posts and missions, a tenuous peace prevailed between two traditional enemies, the Minnesota Dakota and the Lake Superior Ojibwa. In 1731, a French alliance gave the Ojibwa hunting rights west of the St. Croix River, one of the contemporary boundaries between Minnesota and Wisconsin. The Ojibwa were to serve as trading agents for the French with the Dakota, moving furs from their territory to Fort La Pointe on Lake Superior, near today's communities of Ashland and Bayfield, Wisconsin. At this point, there were no permanent Ojibwa settlements west of Lake Superior.

That changed in 1736, when the Dakota killed the French trader and envoy at Fort St. Charles on the southwest shore of Lake of the Woods, along with 19 French voyageurs. The Dakota action provided the excuse sought by the Ojibwa to break their tenuous treaty with the Dakota, and they joined the Cree (who had already lost a fight with the Dakota) in pushing westward. Soon the Ojibwa had established settlements on the Vermilion and Rainy rivers at Thunder Bay. Within four years, they were claiming Rainy Lake and were engaged in open warfare with the Dakota.

A "war zone" or no man's land–eventually it would be 100 miles wide by 400 miles long–was established between the Mississippi River headwaters and Mille Lacs Lake. The Dakota lived in long-established villages on the shores of Sandy Lake, Leech Lake, and Red Lake, waters that contribute to the start of the great river. The Ojibwa moved in, and tribal history tells of the Dakota being forced out by 1745. However, another decade would pass before everything north of the Minnesota River would be considered Ojibwa territory.

The Cree were part of the Algonquian group. Their involvement in what would become the United States would be minimal, but they have always been a major power above that invisible border separating the U.S. from Canada. An estimated 3,000 Cree lived in the Lake of the Woods region at the time of the

Ojibwa ascension.

Although some Native Americans call the timespan between 1492 and 1892 "The Four Hundred Year War," the majority of those years were relatively peaceful in Minnesota. Various wars, from the French and Indian Wars to the American Revolution to the War of 1812, came and went with only minimal involvement on the part of the Indian nations in the Minnesota area. The Ojibwa and the Dakota did send some emissaries, warriors, and negotiators to each of the confrontations, but for the most part, the area had little to do with the shaping of the new American nation.

In 1825, however, the Treaty of Prairie du Chien (Wisconsin) proscribed a specific line that separated the Dakota from the Ojibwa to the north and the Sauk and Mesquakie to the south. These "enforced borders" did not rest well

"Ojibwe Head," a charcoal drawing by American artist Eastman Johnson, who visited the Duluth-Superior area in 1856-57.

with either side, so there were constant conflicts between the traditionally unneighborly nations.

The Removal of Nations

To say the least, President Andrew Jackson's Indian Removal Act of 1830 was not an event celebrated in midwestern Native American communities. The act basically commanded Indians to exchange their homelands, which had already shrunk through treaties, for unknown land west of the Mississippi.

Abrupt removal ensued, except to those few tribes whose orators and lawyers were able to come up with reasons, on a regular basis, to postpone departure. Even then, verbal fights and a few physical fights were lost. Relocation was the goal, and Minnesota presented a kind of conundrum, for it

"Ojibwe Women," by Eastman Johnson.

sat where the Mississippi River began: What were the "legal" limits of the act? What mattered, though, was the fact that supposedly permanent reservations were being established in the year of the Removal Act. Yet for the next thirty years, the U.S. Government would attach further cessions of land to a number of treaties. In 1851, for example, the Traverse des Sioux and Mendota-Dakota ceded all their land in Minnesota for a 20-mile-wide strip of land between Lake Traverse and the Yellow Medicine River. In 1832, the Fox River Winnebago of Wisconsin were moved to a section of land that lay between the Dakota and the Sauk–a most inhospitable neighborhood–and for the next two decades many Winnebago would make their way back to Wisconsin, while others went to stay with the friendly Omaha in Nebraska. In 1848, the U.S. wanted the Menominee out of Wisconsin, so they were moved west to Minnesota, near the Crow Wing River. They would fight extradition until their own tribal entity was successfully reconnected with those Menominee who stayed in Wisconsin.

More Native Americans from Wisconsin were sent west to Minnesota. In 1850, the La Pointe Ojibwa suddenly found their Indian Agency outpost closed, and were told to go to Sandy Lake in Minnesota to receive their annuities. They went. The agent's plan, meanwhile, was to hold them there until winter set in, so he withheld the annuities. Some of the Ojibwa tried to survive in an unknown area, while others tried to walk home. The futility of the situation led to the deaths of 400 Ojibwa. It was part of a concerted effort to combine Ojibwa populations on two reservations, at Leech Lake and White Lake, and finally, in 1889, at Red Lake.

Historical Societies

Many county historical societies in Minnesota offer displays, collections or exhibits devoted to the broad range of Native American lifestyles in the Land of Lakes. What follows is a list of many of these.

The **St. Louis County Historical Museum** in Duluth (506 West Michigan St., 218-722-8011). Admission fee.

Koochiching County Historical Museum, located in the Smokey Bear Park of International Falls (214 Sixth Ave., 218-283-4316). Admission fee.

Lake of the Woods County Museum in Baudette (8th Ave. SE, 218-634-1200) is open from May through September

Roseau County Historical Museum in Roseau (2nd Ave., 218-463-1918).

Otter Tail County Museum in Fergus Falls (1110 Lincoln Ave., 218-736-6038) has a replicated Indian village.

Pope County Historical Museum (Highway 104 South, 809 S. Lakeshore Drive, 612-634-3293) in Glenwood has an artifact collection and a display of daily Indian life.

Grant County Museum in Elbow Lake (Highways 59 and 79).

Crow Wing Historical Museum in Brainerd (20 Laurel St., 218-829-3268).

Brown County Historical Museum in New Ulm (2 North Broadway, 507-354-2016) reflects the Dakota culture as well as the Minnesota Uprising of 1862.

Renville County Historical Museum (Main St., 612-329-3541) in Morton portrays the life of the Dakota people, and nearby is the Tipi Maka Duta Trading Post, where contemporary Santee potters work and where Native American arts and crafts may be purchased.

Mower County Historical Center (12th St. SW) in Austin has an extensive, private collection of arrowheads and spear points.

Rice County Museum in Faribault (1814 NW Second St., 507-332-2121) includes an audio-visual presentation about local history.

Dodge County Historical Society Museum (Highway 57, 507-635-5508) in Mantorville is open from May until October; there is an admission fee.

Goodhue County Historical Museum (1166 Oak St., 612-388-6024) in Red Wing.

Winona County Historical Museum (160 Johnson St., 507-454-2723) in Winona includes Native American exhibits with other Mississippi River historical displays.

Yellow Medicine County Historical Museum (1193 6th St., 612-564-4479) in Granite Falls has "the oldest rock in the world" which, incidentally, is 3.6 billion years old.

McCleod County Historical Museum (380 School Road North, 612-587-2109) in Hutchinson has a statue of Chief Little Crow, and is located near the dam on Highway 15. The sculpture was a gift from noted artist-sculptor Les Kouba.

Kandiyohi County Historical Society Museum (610 Highway 71 NE, 612-235-1881) in Willmar is open from Memorial Day until Labor Day.

Pipestone County Historical Society (113 South Hiawatha) in Mountain Lake has an admission fee.

Displays are also offered at the **Cass County Historical Museum** (218-547-3300); at the **Walker Museum of Natural History** (218-547-1313) in Walker; and at the **Hubbard County Historical Museum** (Old County Courthouse, Court St.) in Park Rapids from June to September.

The Santee and Sibley

In 1862, as the Civil War was building in its terrible intensity, Minnesota's Dakota-Santee faced their own crisis in the land allotted them. The nation found itself surrounded by non-Indian settlements and settlers, and the pressure was on to relinquish their lands–to sell them or trade them. Four young Santee took out their hostility on five settlers by killing them. Afterward, they persuaded the usually peaceful Chief Little Crow to declare war on the non-Indian population, both civilian and military. One of the "last straws" for Little Crow was a cruel statement made by a white trader who refused credit to the long-term, residential Santees, saying, "As far as I am concerned, if they're hungry, let them eat grass!"

The statement became one of the Santee rallying cries. On August 12, 1862, Santees went on raids, killing 400 people on the first day of a series of attacks on towns, trading posts, and even Fort Ridgely. The latter assault was

A haunting Eastman Johnson portrait titled "Notin e Garbowik," or "Standing Wind Woman."

not successful, so Little Crow withdrew his forces. He led his warriors against the fort for two days, but the new weaponry–in this case a battery of howitzers–mowed down more than 100 Santee fighters. On August 23, the Santee attacked the town of New Ulm, but the village was prepared and fought back; one-third of the place was burned down, however.

In September, U.S. General Henry Sibley arrived at Fort Ridgely with a force of 1,500 troops, and on September 2 he sent a 135-man burial party to take care of the bodies of fallen soldiers and settlers. This group was attacked by Little Crow, but by ringing their wagons, the burial party survived the siege for a day and a half, until help came from the fort. Two weeks later Sibley, who followed the retreating Santee, confronted 700 of Chief Little Crow's warriors and defeated them. Little Crow went to Canada with some of his forces, while others headed for the Dakota Territory to the west.

More than 300 Santee were captured, and all were condemned to death. President Lincoln reviewed the individual cases–he had been a captain in the Illinois militia during the so-called Black Hawk War three decades earlier–and commuted all but 38 sentences. On the day after Christmas in 1862, the biggest mass execution in U.S. history took place, as all 38 were hanged simultaneously. Little Crow himself was killed in the summer of 1863, as he led a successful raid out of Canada in quest of horses. Settlers shot him and turned in his scalp, with those of the other dead, for a bounty being paid on Santee scalp locks.

The persistent Gen. Sibley tracked the other Santee into the Dakota Territory and defeated them along with some Teton-Lakota allies at Big Mound, Dead Buffalo Lake, and Stoney Lake. A year later, another U.S. force defeated the two tribes at Whitestone Hill and Killdeer Mountain. In 1865, however, the Santee-Teton alliance would avenge their losses farther west.

Historical Attractions

There is a **Sibley State Park** in the Minnesota River Valley, and one of its featured attractions is Mt. Tom, which rises only 150 feet above the lake below but is the highest point for 50 miles. It was once used as a Dakota ceremonial site.

Pipestone National Monument (Hwy 75, 507-825-5464) is a stone quarry that is still being used by Native Americans for the fabrication and creation of pipes and other ceremonial or sacred objects. There is an Upper Midwestern Cultural Center in the park, and for three weekends during the summer, "The Song of Hiawatha" is performed in an outdoor amphitheater.

The **Lower Sioux Agency** (Cty Rd 2, 507-697-6321) near Morton is open from May until September. Part of the agency's original warehouse is still intact, and displays "focus on the Dakota Indians as they faced the loss of their traditional lands to pioneer settlement."

A layer of the stone that earned Pipestone National Monument its name.

The Grand Mound History Center, offering information on Minnesota's Laurel Indians.

The Grand Mound–Minnesota's largest prehistoric earthwork.

In Granite Falls, the **Upper Sioux Agency** (Hwy 67, 612-564-4777) features another warehouse, surviving from 1854, and the **Upper Sioux Agency State Park** has a natural history interpretive museum.

The Era of Allotments

From 1862 on, the Santee who remained in Minnesota were contained within small reservations along the Minnesota River. This was the era in which "allotments" of land were provided to Native Americans still living in Minnesota and other states. The function of the land allotment practice was to allow settlement of individual Indian landholders in 40- and 80-acre plots. Two things were accomplished: First, the communal nature of Indian farming and subsistence was broken up; second, the division of the land into sections allowed land brokers and ambitious non-Indian settlers to buy sections from their designated owners. The surviving Santee took their 80-acre allotments on the old Minnesota River reservation, but more than 350 Santee were landless, living in clusters around Faribault, Mendota, near Redwood Falls, Yellow Medicine River, Wabasha, and Big Stone Lake. Essentially, the allotment practice was the government's way of quickly dissolving tribal integrity and cultural cohesion. Allotted land could be–and was–subsequently sold or stolen.

The quest for land was unceasing, for by the time Minnesota became a state in 1858, there were nearly 500,000 non-Indians within its boundaries. The Ojibwa population was estimated at around 7,000 people living north of the Minnesota River. Some Native American communities were centered around a particular church, as in the case of White Earth, which was Episcopalian, and Grand Portage, which was Catholic.

Development of a railroad line from St. Paul to Breckenridge linked the Red River to the southern trade routes, to the Mississippi River and by railway to Chicago and points west. That was in place by 1871. An agreement between Canada and the U.S. in 1870 also abolished the Hudson Bay Company's previous role as a governing entity in northern Minnesota and Canada, affecting more than 7,000 Indians in both countries.

By the turn of the 20th century, present-day reservations were basically established, although the non-Indians would continue to buy away tribal lands. Still, Minnesota today contains a number of the largest reservations in the United States.

Reservations

The **Fond du Lac Reservation** lies within Carlton and St. Louis counties, and is an Ojibwa reservation headquartered in Cloquet. The reservation covers about 21,000 acres, and the **Fond du Lac Reservation Business Committee** (105 University Ave., 218-879-1251) serves about 1,500 members.

The reservation has its **Fond-du-Luth Gaming Casino** (East Superior Street, 218-722-0280) in Duluth, which offers Las Vegas-style gaming as well as bingo and other games.

The **Grand Portage Reservation** is an Ojibwa reservation in Cook County that occupies 44,000 acres. The **Grand Portage Reservation Business Committee** (218-475-2277) serves more than 325 members of the band. Camping is available on the reservation in three remote areas. Some units include water and toilet facilities, as well as marina and trailer access.

The **Leech Lake Reservation** of the Ojibwa is located in Beltrami, Cass, Hubbard, and Itasca counties, covering 27,700 acres with tribal headquarters located in Cass Lake. The band is administered by the **Minnesota Chippewa Tribe** (218-335-2252). The **Leech Lake Bingo Palace** (Resort Area Drive, 800-228-6676 or 218-335-6787) is situated in Cass Lake and offers high-stakes bingo year-round.

The **Lower Sioux Reservation** is in Redwood County, and is a 1700-acre reservation. It's governed by the **Lower Sioux Community Council** (507-697-6416/6185) in Morton, which serves 215 members.

The **Upper Sioux Reservation** is located in Yellow Medicine County near

An array of Ojibwa bead necklaces

Granite Falls. The 750-acre reservation is governed by the **Upper Sioux Board of Trustees** (612-564-4504), representing the interests of 135 members.

The **Prior Lake Reservation** is a Sioux reservation in Carver County, governed by the **Shakopee Business Council** (612-564-4504). **Little Six Bingo** (2350 Sioux Trail NW, 612-445-9000) in Prior Lake is operated by the Mdewakanton Sioux. Buses serving the casino run from Minneapolis to Prior Lake.

The **Mille Lacs Reservation** is located in Mille Lacs, Aitkin, and Pine counties, with tribal headquarters in Onamia (612-532-4181). The **Mille Lacs Reservation Business Committee** oversees the 3600-acre reservation's activities, and serves the needs of the 915 Ojibwa band members. The **Mille Lacs Indian Museum** (Highway 169, 612-532-3632) in Onamia features life-size dioramas depicting the daily life of the Ojibwa through the four seasons, and offers Dakota displays as well. The museum is open from May through September. There is also a Mille Lacs **Kathio State Park** including Ogechie Lake and Rum River. Kathio was the main village of the Dakota people in the 18th century, before Ojibwa domination of Minnesota occurred. The park is open year-round.

Ojibwa baskets, made in various sizes from birchbark.

Visitors examine an Oneida Longhouse

The **Prairie Island Reservation** in Goodhue County is a 530-acre reservation with 125 members. Its tribal office in Welch is overseen by the **Prairie Island Community Council** (612-388-8889), and the tribe also operates **Island Bingo** (County Road 18, 800-222-7077 in MN or 800-822-4529 elsewhere), located 15 miles north of Red Wing on Sturgeon Lake Road. Las Vegas-style gaming is offered here.

Minnesota's largest reservation is the **Red Lake Reservation**, containing more than 630,000 acres and a population of 4,500 Ojibwa. The reservation is served by the **Red Lake Tribal Council** (218-679-3343). Red Lake offers visitors camping at Sandy Beach, and a number of units have water and toilets. Forty-five picnic sites and free firewood are also available. There is a fee for camping. Contact the Red Lake Reservation for information or reservations.

The **Nett Lake Reservation** is an Ojibwa reservation of 1,000 members, served by the **Bois Forte Business Committee** (218-757-3261).

The **White Earth Reservation** in Mahonmen, Becker and Clearwater counties has its headquarters in Ponsford, and elects the **White Earth Reservation Business Council** (218-935-5956).

Agencies and Organizations

In Minneapolis, the **American Indian Center** (1530 East Franklin Ave., 612-871-4555) works to ensure the social and economic development of Native Americans in Minneapolis through health, education, recreational, senior, and youth programs. The center operates the Two Rivers Gallery, which features work by regional artists, as well as the Glass Wigwam Gift Store and the Circle Cafe. The center maintains the Mino-Aki grounds and publishes a monthly newspaper entitled *The Circle*.

The **Upper Midwest American Indian Center** (1113 West Broadway, 612-522-4436) is also located in Minneapolis, and houses more than 500 volumes in its library dealing with the Indians of the northern plains.

In St. Paul, Native American organizations include the **Twin Cities Chippewa Council** (1592 Hoyt Ave. East), the **St. Paul American Indian Center** (1001 Payne Ave., 612-776-8592), and the **Ira Hayes Friendship House** (1671 Summit Ave.).

The **American Indian Movement** (AIM) was founded in Minneapolis in 1968 by three Ojibwa–Dennis Banks, George Mitchell, and Clyde Bellcourt–and a Sioux, Russell Means, to encourage self-determination and to establish international recognition of treaty rights. AIM also founded the **Heart of the**

Evening dancers at a festival.

Earth Survival School and maintains historical archives, provides speakers, and conducts research. The organization has participated in numerous protests and demonstrations, advocating justice and Native American rights. There are now offices in San Francisco and Indianapolis, and AIM has maintained one in Minneapolis (1208 Fourth St. SE, 612-379-1550).

The **National Indian Education Association** (1115 Second Ave. South) is located in Minneapolis and has been designing programs for improving the social and economic well-being of Native Americans and Native Alaskans through education for more than two decades.

In Duluth, the **American Indian Fellowship Association** (8 East Second St.) is an active organization.

MIGIZI Communications, Inc. (3123 East Lake St., Suite 200, 612-721-6631) in Minneapolis works to provide a national American Indian news service for radio and television, seeking a balanced presentation for Indian and non-Indian journalists. A weekly news program is produced, and young women of high school age are provided media training.

In St. Paul the **Grotto Foundation, Inc.** (West-2090 First National Bank Building, 612-224-9431) provides grants for special projects relating to American Indians.

The **Minnesota Area Office of the Bureau of Indian Affairs** (15 South Fifth St., Tenth Floor, 612-349-3391) administers reservations and programs for Iowa, Michigan, and Wisconsin, as well as Minnesota.

Libraries

A number of libraries offer extensive Native American collections. The **Becker County Historical Society Library** (915 Lake Ave.) in Detroit Lakes has a collection including 1,500 volumes about the White Earth Reservation, which covers 12 townships in Becker Country.

The **Minneapolis College of Art and Design's Learning Resource Center** (200 East 25th St.) contains "The American Indian Book Collection."

The **Minnesota Historical Society Audio-Visual Library** (690 Cedar St., 612-296-2489) in St. Paul includes more than 30 films from the 1930s through the 1950s, with recent additions from the Ojibwa and other Minnesota peoples, as well as Blackfeet materials. The Historical Society's **Division of Archives and Manuscripts** (1500 Mississippi St., 612-296-6980) in St. Paul has a significant collection of materials dealing with the Ojibwa and Dakota peoples, plus material about the Winnebago. The division also has information about Indian education, state census schedules, and correspondence regarding Indian affairs in the Governor's papers.

Renowned dancer Ray Cadotte leads others at an Oneida powwow.

Education

There are at least four Native American schools on Minnesota reservations. At Cass Lake, the **Chief Bug-o-nay-ge Shig School** (218-665-2282) covers kindergarten through 12th grade. The **Fond du Lac Ojibwa School** (218-879-4593) in Cloquet also instructs students from kindergarten through 12th grade. On the Mille Lacs Reservation, the **Nay Ah Shing School** (612-532-4181) in Onamia covers seventh through twelfth grades, with an emphasis on Native American studies. And on the White Earth Reservation, students attend the **Circle of Life Survival School** (218-983-3285, ext. 269).

A number of institutions of higher learning in Minnesota offer Native American studies programs or courses. **Bemidji State University** (218-755-2032) in Bemidji has an American Indian studies department. **Fond du Lac Community College** (105 University Road, 218-879-02441) in Cloquet offers a variety of courses in Native American subjects. The **College of St. Scholastica** (1200 Kenwood Ave.) in Duluth has a department of American Indian studies, as does the **University of Minnesota-Duluth** (2400 Oakland Ave.).

Augsburg College (612-330-1138) in Minneapolis offers an American Indian Support Program, which provides direct assistance, counseling, and advocacy. An American Indian Studies minor has been proposed there, and the support program is connected to a number of community and tribal agencies, including the Minneapolis American Indian Center, the Indian Health Board, and the Minnesota Indian Women's Resource Center. The program also works through reservation educational systems and the departments of education for Minnesota, Minneapolis, and St. Paul.

Minneapolis Community College (1501 Hennepin Ave.) has a social sciences/American Indians department. The **University of Minnesota** (612-625-3400) in Minneapolis has departments of American Indian Studies and archaeology. And **Moorhead State University** (11th Street South) in Moorhead has a department of Indian Studies.

A dancer at the Stand Rock Ceremonial, near Wisconsin Dells.

1 .... Becker County Historical Society
2 .... Brown County Historical Society
3 .... Crow Wing County Historical Society
4 .... Dodge County Historical Society
5 .... Fond du Lac
6 .... Goodhue County Historical Society
7 .... Grand Mound History Center
8 .... Grand Portage Reservation
9 .... Grand Portage National Monument
10 .... Grant County Historical Society
11 .... Jeffers Petroglyphs
12 .... Kandiyohi County Historical Society
13 .... Kathio State Park
14 .... Koochiching County Historical Society
15 .... Lake of the Woods County Historical Society
16 .... Leech Lake Reservation
17 .... Lower Sioux Reservation
18 .... McCleod County Historical Society
19 .... Mille Lacs Reservation
20 .... Mounds Park
21 .... Mower County Historical Society
22 .... Nett Lake
23 .... North West Company Fur Trading Post
24 .... Otter Tail County Historical Society
25 .... Pipestone County Historical Society
26 .... Pipestone National Monument
27 .... Pope County Historical Society
28 .... Prairie Island Reservation
29 .... Prior Lake Reservation
30 .... Red Lake Reservation
31 .... Renville County Historical Society
32 .... Rice County Historical Society
33 .... Roseau County Historical Society
34 .... Upper Sioux Reservation
35 .... Upper Sioux Agency State Park
36 .... Vermillion Interpretive Center
37 .... White Earth Reservation
38 .... Winona County Historical Society
39 .... Yellow Medicine County Historical Society

Native Minnesota

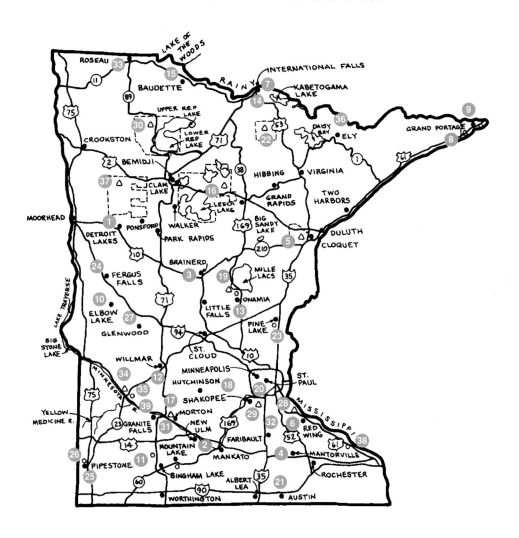

△ Reservations

● Attractions &
Historic Sites

● Cities & Towns

--- Reservation
Boundaries

Conclusion:
Our Travels and Yours

Accumulating the information contained in this initial volume of the "Origins" series involved many months--in some cases, years--of locating sources, visiting museums, parks, reservations, and other institutions. While there may be no other guide quite like this one, it would be inappropriate to assume that what lies between these covers is definitive. It's important, therefore, to make a few concluding points.

If there are errors in the text, please accept apologies. We have made every attempt to be accurate, but telephone numbers and addresses inevitably change. Some commercial enterprises dissolve. Museums and libraries may change their perspective on Native Americans, one way or another. Collections may change as a result of Native American objection to the display of bones, figures, and sacred objects. These objects may be returned to Mother Earth and the Spirit World.

Some of the collections described in the text simply as "archaeological artifacts" might indeed be profoundly offensive to American Indians, or may be displayed in such a way as to demean the cultural integrity of Indian people. When we attempted to understand the "style" or perspective of several historical societies, for example, we received calm assurances that everything was being presented in a respectful manner. But that is a matter of judgment, and even respectfully-intended displays may offend some sensibilities.

Reader-traveler response to the guide is welcomed, and should be addressed to NorthWord Press, P.O. Box 1360, Minocqua, WI 54548. We hope the demand for *Traveler's Guide* will necessitate future editions. If so, we'll have an opportunity to incorporate new information, corrected data, proper spellings, and most importantly, clarification of any misinterpretations of history or culture.

Traveler's Guide was not a book designed or written to be read like a novel or a history book, so readers looking for a consistent style of presentation will find instead a coat of many colors. Each state is different in personality and history, and so the information available to the traveler varies as well. Wherever possible, we have attempted to stay within a framework of time and place, but there are occasions when the past and the present--in Wisconsin, for example--provide so much information from so many different angles that the chapter may appear to be a multi-faceted stone.

In her preface, Pemina Yellow Bird provided cogent points about non-Indian attitudes and behavior while visiting sites, ceremonies, and communities. In the diplomatic world, this concern is called "protocol," meaning rules governing the proper way to behave in particular situations. While we have mentioned

Petroglyphs created by non-Indian stone masons in Illinois, in honor of their Potawatomi neighbors.

189

such considerations briefly in other places, it might be appropriate to conclude this guide with a few reminders.

When on a reservation or near a place considered sacred, as in the case of mounds, be respectful. As Pemina suggests, a bikini is not appropriate attire at a powwow or in a cultural center. Visitors should not take offense, any more than they would upon reading a sign that advises, "No shoes, no shirt, no service."

How does one learn what to do or wear in such situations? Common sense is your best guide, and some reservations even provide printed suggestions, recommendations, or prohibitions. At powwows, for example, there are standing rules against consumption of alcohol or use of drugs. Some powwow announcers will ask that, at certain moments of homage, children be silent as well as adults. There are moments in a powwow when an individual and his or her family is honored by a special song, and they are the only ones dancing. Other dancers stand in the circle as a sign of respect, and the audience is often asked to stand as well.

Some reservations prohibit photography at particular events, but the visitor is generally advised of such prohibitions. Sacred moments are not times for recording, and it's interesting to note that, in the early days of photography, men with cameras were called "Shadow Catchers." Most powwows do not allow pets to accompany audience members—and for good reason, since a dog fight is not only dangerous but also disruptive to the dancing. The bodily functions of pets can also cause unpleasantness.

Non-residents and non-tribal members may not be permitted in certain areas of a reservation. Signs are usually posted to warn people away, but if a visitor is asked to leave, he or she should graciously comply with the request. Spirit places are holy, and only those "qualified" may be there, because they understand the beliefs and know what behavior is expected.

Living conditions on reservations are not what one might find in America's middle-class suburbs, yet value judgments are inappropriate here, just as they are when visiting any other culture. Stopping the car to take a picture of someone's yard, or stopping to point and make gestures from behind closed windows, demonstrates insensitivity and communicates a very different message than the one this book hopes to facilitate.

Believe it or not, tourists of all races and nationalities are joked about and disdained throughout the world. Travelers, on the other hand, are regarded differently, for they are usually open-minded, generous to a fault, and conscious of the feelings of others. If one pauses to consider all the cartoons that portray the "typical" tourist, then looks in the mirror and finds the same sort of image, perhaps the notion of becoming a traveler may in itself be a worthy goal.

If, on the other hand, one looks into the mirror and sees a kind and curious human being, a person slightly surprised that he or she is not entirely invisible, then experiencing the fascinating aspects of Native American culture will be educational and delightful.

We look forward to seeing you on your next visit to our "Origins."

A miniature collision of cultures: Traditional clothing and contemporary popcorn.

Sources and Select Bibliography

As one might imagine, there have been countless books and other materials written about the Native American culture, heritage, and experience. Each of the following books has been helpful in the formulation of this guide, as well as providing access to extensive bibliographies that deal with myriad subjects, geographical areas, and tribal nations or histories.

Atlas of Great Lakes Indian History. Edited by Helen Hornbeck Tanner. University of Oklahoma Press, 1987.

Brandon, William. *The American Heritage Book of Indians.* Dell, 1973.

Eagle/Walking Turtle. *Indian America.* John Muir Publications, 1989.

Folsom, Franklin and Mary E. *America's Ancient Treasures.* University of New Mexico Press, 1983.

Lurie, Nancy Ostereich. *Wisconsin Indians.* State Historical Society of Wisconsin, 1987.

Marquis, Arnold. *A Guide to America's Indians.* University of Oklahoma Press, 1987.

Native American Directory. National Native American Cooperative, 1982.

Reference Encyclopedia of the American Indian. Edited by Barry T. Klein. Todd Publications, 1990.

Stoutenburg, John Jr. *Dictionary of the American Indian.* Bonanza Books, 1990.

The World of the American Indian. Edited by Jules B. Billard. National Geographic, 1974.

Waldman, Carl. *Atlas of the North American Indian.* Facts on File, 1985.

Waldman, Carl. *Encyclopedia of Native American Tribes.* Facts on File, 1988.

It should be noted that the Wisconsin Department of Public Instruction, under the auspices of the American Indian Language and Culture Education Board, has published a comprehensive and inexpensive set of teacher's manuals that deal with Wisconsin Indian history, Indian-white relations, specific tribal histories, and governing structures. The individual editions were particularly valuable in presenting tribal perspectives regarding their histories and their contemporary concerns.